PRAISE FOR MIKE CAROTTA

"We read books for all kinds of reasons. Learning to fish is not the reason to read *A Long Cast*. Learning why we go fishing certainly is. Anyone who spends many consecutive days and nights surfcasting on the beach as Mike Carotta did for 50 years will learn a lot about themselves and those they meet. *A Long Cast* is a compendium of those warm memories that keep us going through the offseason and keep us coming back to those places we love. This is not about the fish we catch, but about the people who have been caught by the fish in a magical place."

> – RIP CUNNINGHAM,
> former Editor-In-Chief and
> Publisher of Salt Water
> Sportsman magazine,
> an inductee into the
> Fishing Hall of Fame
> and a friend of the fish

"For readers who like stories told straight from the heart, without polish or pretense. If you've ever stood in your own version of the surf, whether that's a kitchen, a church, or a backyard garden, you'll find yourself in these pages. ... By the end, I wasn't thinking about fishing at all. I was thinking about family traditions, about the way landscapes hold onto us, about how we carry certain people with us long after they're gone."

– LITERARY TITAN

A LONG CAST

A LONG CAST

REFLECTIONS ON 50 YEARS OF VISITING THE MARTHA'S VINEYARD SURF

MIKE CAROTTA

Vista, CA

Copyright © 2023 Mike Carotta

All rights reserved. Torchflame Books supports copyright. Copyright fuels creativity, encourages diverse voices, promotes free speech, and creates a vibrant culture. Thank you for buying an authorized edition of this book and for complying with copyright laws by not reproducing, scanning, or distributing any part of it in any form without permission, except by a reviewer who wishes to quote brief passages in connection with a review written for insertion in a magazine, newspaper, broadcast, website, blog or other outlet. You are supporting independent publishing and allowing Torchflame Books to publish books for all readers.

NO AI TRAINING: Without in any way limiting the author's [and publisher's] exclusive rights under copyright, any use of this publication to "train" generative artificial intelligence (AI) technologies to generate text is expressly prohibited. The author reserves all rights to license uses of this work for generative AI training and development of machine learning language models.

ISBN: 978-1-61153-711-6

Library of Congress Control Number: 2023904618

A Long Cast: Reflections on 50 years of visiting the Martha's Vineyard surf is published in 2025 by: Torchflame Books Large Print, an imprint of Top Reads Publishing, LLC, 1035 E. Vista Way, Suite 205, Vista, CA 92084, USA

www.torchflamebooks.com/large-print

The publisher is not responsible for websites or social media accounts (or their content) that are not owned by the publisher.

Cover Design by Wally Turnbull

Interior Design by Jori Hanna

Cover photo courtesy Benjamin Carotta

This Large Print Edition is set in 16-point Iowan Old Style type.

CONTENTS

Introduction	xv

PART ONE
DISCOVERING THE ISLAND

Finding Your Place	3
Liminal Space	10
Getting It Right	16
Befriending the Place	24

PART TWO
THIRTY STRAIGHT

Week One: May 18-24	35
Jigging	41
Shore Birds	51
Ruin Things	66
Log Day	71
Week Two: May 25-31	79
The Tug	85
The Car	91
This Humbles You	98
Re-Tie	106
Can't Eat as Much	112
Week Three: June 1-7	121
Pivoting	127
The Opening	133

The Cast	139
Mom and Dad Days	143
Tribute	148
Farewell and Thank You	154
Week Four: June 8-15	164
The Envelope	170
Catching Beauty	177
Gratitude	182
Seeing the Unseen	190
The Power of Gesture	198
Fishing With Ghosts	204

PART THREE
WHAT REMAINS

The Fishing Partner	211
The Last Day	216
My Biggest Keeper	225
Acknowledgments	243
About the Author	245
Thank You!	247

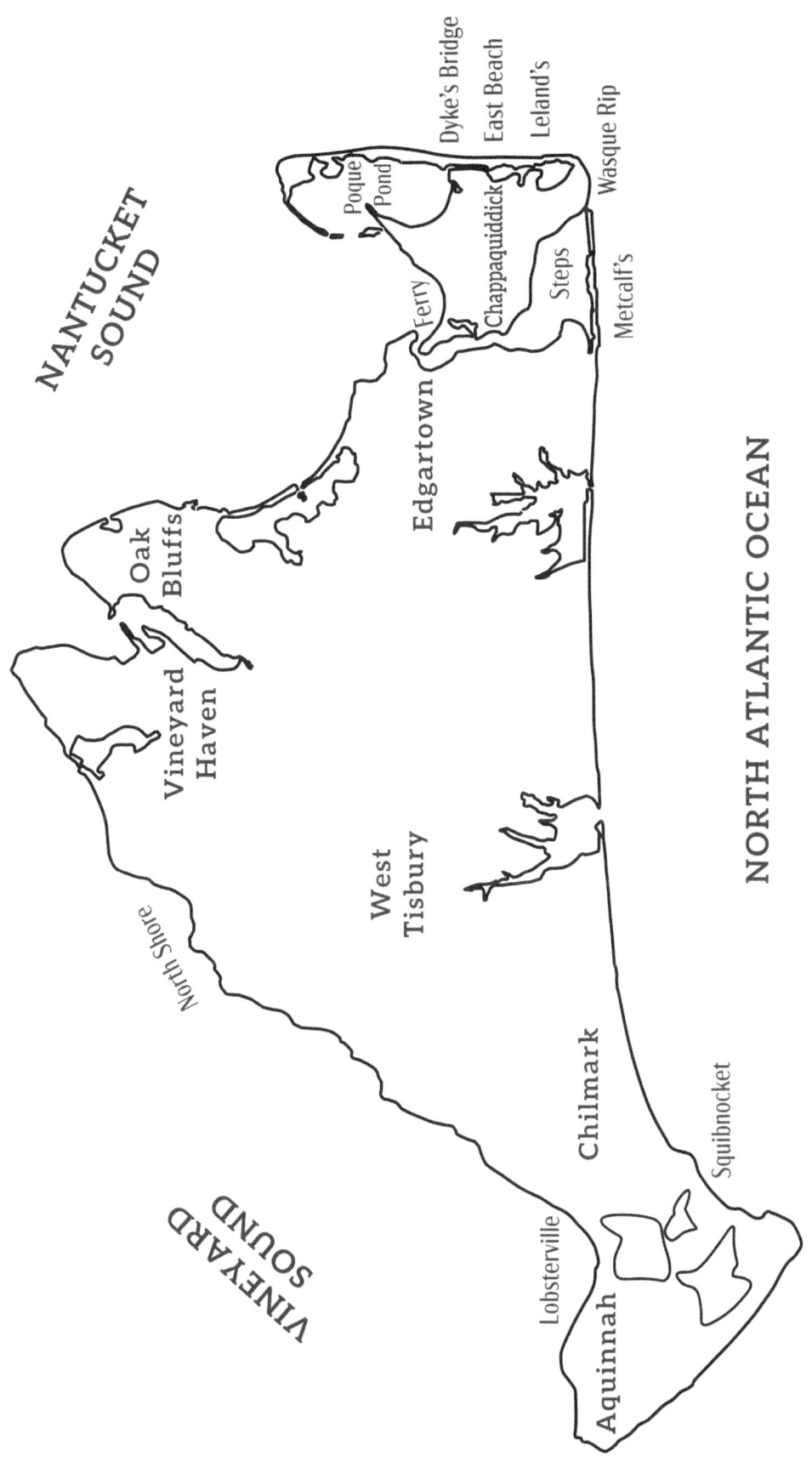

Years from now when a lot of those mentioned in this book are gone, friends and family still around might find in these pages a way to recall the wonderful times we had when we were all together.

INTRODUCTION

I am not a good surf fisherman.

    I ought to be a whole lot better than I am after fishing fifty-one annual Spring runs in the surf of Martha's Vineyard with each trip ranging from two to four weeks long.

    There are no helpful fishing hints here.

    I say this upfront in case you are hoping this book may provide you some surf casting tips or secrets.

    This is a collection of recollection: stories of saltwater characters, occurrences, and conversations. Like stars in the night sky, they are best enjoyed when you get some distance from the lights of other stuff.

Since I just turned seventy, I thought I would try to put my waders in the water thirty straight days and nights. I know I will never have another chance to do so. I will keep an informal track of things and share it with you—without the technical issues we fishermen put in our logs, like wind speed and direction, time of tide, etc.

I am writing this Introduction before I get to the water. I suspect the fish will not be in abundance. Last year, after twenty-one nights and days on the water, I was able to catch just three striped bass of legal size. I did not catch a bluefish for the first seventeen days.

But I know the nights in the water will bring back to life old fishing memories I plan to record.

More than anything, I hope that somehow this may bring to mind some of your favorite recreational memories and take you back to where some things are once again clear, true, noble, and restorative.

And the distance between heaven and earth gets a little thinner.

PART ONE
DISCOVERING THE ISLAND

FINDING YOUR PLACE

The best thing about fishing.
Something I thought to include in this book.

I'll get to that later.

Right now, our lures are snapping off on every other cast.

When they don't snap off, the bluefish in front of us are biting through the line anyway. This has been going on for an hour.

After a morning of exploring Martha's Vineyard, we found the tiny island on The Island called Chappaquiddick and a fishing spot we could not pronounce: Wasque (Way Squee).

I have just finished my freshmen year in

college and have never surf casted before. My dad had been to the Bass Derby here on Martha's Vineyard in the mid '50s and was smitten. We came here in a station wagon we borrowed from my uncle Sammy. We had to push it on the ferry in Woods Hole because it kept stalling.

We slid down a cliff here on Wasque and walked through a lagoon called Swan Pond to get to the ocean.

Dad brought the very same rods he had used in the '50s: *wooden* bamboo surf rods as stiff as a broom handle. The fishing line is nylon. We have conventional reels. You cast with your thumb on the spool to keep it from making a mess. He has forgotten how to tie a knot. We don't know anything about metal leaders to fend off bluefish biting through the ancient nylon fishing line.

After watching us lose everything, the one lone fisherman here at Wasque Point stops to give us some lures, leaders, and a tutorial on how to tie a proper clinch knot.

It is 1971.

We both caught bluefish.

"Can we eat these?" I asked.

The thought of catching food out of the ocean

in front of you impressed me beyond words and has abided in me ever since.

Our plan was to visit Martha's Vineyard and then head to the Cape Cod town of Orleans where I had heard the fishing was good. After Wasque we got back on the Ferry and headed back to the mainland. Standing on the rail, looking at the emerald blue-green water for thirty minutes, we never said a word.

We checked in on each other just before the Ferry pulled into Woods Hole:

"Why are we going to Orleans?"

"To see how good the fishing is."

"It can't be better than where we just were."

"You're right."

So, we got back on the Ferry and spent our entire two weeks fishing the Vineyard.

That's how it began.

We slept in the station wagon at Webb's Campground every Spring for about three years, including the Spring I volunteered us to be extras in some film called *Jaws*.

One spring we slept side by side in the station wagon for a month. Side by side. Cooking breakfast on a green Coleman camping stove. Taking showers every couple of days in the locker room.

We lived off salami sandwiches and tomato rice soup which we heated up in this glass mug that had a heating coil in it. You plugged it in to your cigarette lighter and you had hot soup or hot chocolate.

While campers in tents got washed out in a strong and long rain, we were off the ground and dry. We had it made.

Every night, as I fell asleep in the wagon, my dad would spend thirty minutes sitting at a wood picnic table with his flat rectangular cassette tape player listening to songs by Jerry Vale and Jimmy Roselli.

In Italian.

We were in Webb's Campground, but I knew that the Italian music took my immigrant dad someplace else. I can only imagine what the other campers back in the Woodstock era of the early '70s were thinking.

Today, I smile every time I hear the current generation of immigrants playing the music of their native tongue on their radios while working on construction sites or sitting around in their yard on a Sunday afternoon.

Dad and I fished every spring together on the

Island for almost thirty years. I believe it extended his life.

Our passions have a way of doing that for us: extending our lives.

For him, the cold winters were filled with long conversations on how we would approach the next Spring Run. We would spend hours on the phone discussing which spot and which lures and what time of the tide to go where next Spring.

He was the best fishing partner I ever had.

Our three children grew up fishing the Spring run with us and have great memories as well. They are now grown and two of them make the trip every Spring. Our daughter Christin calls the whole thing "Enchanted." Our youngest son Ben dreams all year of a better lure to solve the riddle of catching finicky stripers that can slap the top of the water in front of you for hours without ever saying hello to whatever you are fishing with.

Our oldest son Aaron used to say fishing with Grandpa was like fishing with a guide who would rig you up, stand next to you in the right spot, and open some raw clams for you on the tailgate for lunch.

My mom took note the last time the roles were reversed and Aaron carefully and lovingly helped his seventy-five-year-old grandpa put on *his* waders.

Other fishermen have enjoyed watching the kids grow from year to year and the kids themselves have come to cherish their time with the collection of characters that migrate to the Island from multiple states every May to fish all day for blues and bass.

Now, as adults with busy and complex lives like all of us, our kids immediately find a quiet spot in the surf and go into that space where, in solitude, each can review the prior year, sort out the important things that lie in the year ahead, and breathe.

Ben, upon leaving to go back to California recently, hugged me and said: "Thanks for the Reset."

I suspect we all have Found Our Place.

Literally.

For some of us it's a coffee shop, the kitchen of a loved one, a health club, a summer garden, a college campus, a vacation spot, a bench in a special park, or the ole neighborhood.

But many have not been able to spend enough time with that place.

My wife once shared this from the late

theologian poet John O'Donohue's book *Beauty: The Invisible Embrace*. He wrote:

> Is it not possible that a place can have huge affection for those who dwell there? Perhaps your place loves having you there. It misses you when you are away and in its secret way rejoices when you return. Could it be that a landscape might have a deep friendship with you? That it could sense your presence and feel the care you extend towards it?

You know it is completely possible when you Find Your Place.

We never ever made it to Orleans.

LIMINAL SPACE

You know those Moments when the distance between heaven and earth suddenly is not so far apart?

Those Moments when a little bit of heaven makes itself plain?

The ancients called it the liminal space.

In the liminal space there is new understanding. And illumination. And maybe even some inspiration.

The elderly fellow sitting on a bolder in Aquinnah back at the start of this long cast fifty years ago made it clear that we would—if we dared—find fishing here to be liminal space.

Dick Morris, who started Dick's Tackle Shop in Oaks Bluff, and whose Derby hall of fame fishermen grandson Steve Morris maintains so very well today, gave us directions and instruction as to where to go and how to fish Gay Head, now called Aquinnah, back in 1971 on our very first trip.

That evening, around dusk, we stumbled our way to the spot Dick Morris told us to go.

There we found a solitary elder perched alone on a boulder like a mystic living on the proverbial mountaintop. Owen Rabbitt Sr. introduced himself and straight away waxed philosophically and spiritually about the life lessons he had learned living on this Island, the fishing 'round here, and what was possible for those who would put in the time doing the hard work of befriending it.

He spoke for forty-five minutes to us strangers as we stood there with our rods in our hands. We said not a word, save a careful question here and there. Years later, whenever recalling the encounter, Dad would utter something he never ever said about anyone else: "That man was full of wisdom."

Forty-five minutes later, two more Island

fishermen arrived. We fished near them, but not next to them.

The sun went down, the moon came up.

The moon went down, and the sun came up.

Hear this: not a word was spoken among any of them, nor us, the entire time.

They had a few hook ups but no bass were landed.

Those two other fishermen were a young Bernie Arruda and Cooper Gilkes. Dad and I came back the very next night and did it again. And Bernie Arruda returned.

We came back to that spot the very next year. Fished sundown, through the entire night, to sunrise again. At dawn on the first day of our second year, I caught my first striper. Broke the old bamboo rod setting the hook.

Looking back, I see that encountering that lone and revered Islander Owen Rabbitt was an omen, an announcement, a heads-up. He was telling us two things that proved to be most true:

1. Come correct. Fishing here takes knowledge. Fish the right lure the right way at the right place.

2. What you catch in this place will enrich you far more than fish. The lone elder on that rock up in Gay Head made it clear: This place has the ability to show you things deeper than fishing: things seen and heard in liminal space.

You learn to notice when the person fishing next to you is in that liminal space. It is actually quite common.

See how he or she is silently casting without saying a word for forty-five minutes. See how someone you might not know begins a conversation about some deeper observation or memory that has nothing to do with the fishing.

See how fishermen spend time alone even while in a group. How she or he drifts down the beach alone with her or his thoughts.

Surf casting is a wall-to-wall sensual experience. Maybe that's what helps shrink the distance between heaven and earth.

The sound of the waves—sometimes lapping up on the shore, sometimes crashing with force, most times methodically rolling into the shore and back out. The sounds of the wind. The sounds of the birds. The sounds of the shells and pebbles tumbling in the wash of the waves.

The sights, the unforgettable sights that transcend those we see back home. The color of the water. The cloud cover. The approaching storm. The glorious sun-soaked sand and sea in front of you. The way the sun rises on the sea. The stars in the night sky, and my favorite, the light of the full moon shining from a black sky illuminating the black sea like a streetlight and casting your shadow on the beach behind you.

The feeling of the cold salt water on your hands, pressed against the legs of your waders. The force of the sea coming up on you in the surf and then from behind you on its way back out. The way your body still rocks gently to that rhythm while you lay in bed at night after five to six days in the surf.

The way your hands hurt. The myriad of line cuts on your fingers. The new callouses on your hands. The way you can't stand up straight after a while. The ache in your shoulder. The lovely and satisfying tiredness after a day or night in the water.

Maybe it is the way the body receives all this that helps bring the heart and the mind to the liminal space found in surf fishing here on The Island.

All of us find liminal space in our own ways. Some of us go there on vacation, others find it unplanned. Some of us get there through specific practices, or celebrations, or writers, or artists, or songs, or get-togethers.

And you know when you are there, right?

First bass. Gay Head 1972. Note wooden Bamboo rod (taped where broken).

GETTING IT RIGHT

He just took the cigar out of his mouth and burned the other's guy's line.

Holy cow.

In the early days of the '70s and '80s Martha's Vineyard was not Celebrity Central. The island was a blue-collar community of women and men trying to keep themselves and their families afloat year-round in a place that had no business in the Winter.

Locals like to say that over the last two decades, the Island went from gravel to glitz.

Back then there used to be epic runs of large muscular bluefish and hefty striped bass and even large weakfish from Memorial Day through maybe the Fourth of July. We always tried to fish the last week of May and the first week of June.

Some guys fished the beach to supplement their day jobs. You could sell fish directly to restaurants and fish markets on the Island back then, so the Spring Run was a source of income.

These guys did not play. They never said much.

You could fish near them if you came correct. If you fished too slow or cast in the wrong direction you would get a look. If you crossed their lines more than once they would cut your line so they would not have to get tangled up with you and slow down the action.

Or burn your line.

They were never mean. But they did not play. And for the first ten to twelve Springs, most of them guarded what they knew and did not share it freely.

And we learned everything from them. The same things the new generation of surfcasters already seems to know and practice:

- Proper protocol of walking down the beach in the direction the fish is running after you hooked it so that you

would walk "underneath the other fisherman" down the beach and out of the way.
- The best time of the tide to fish this spot and that one.
- How and when to use a leader.
- The most appropriate speed of retrieve for different types of lures.
- When the County would be opening a tidal pond to the sea via bulldozers—thus spilling the Pond's bait into the surf where the bass lay in wait.
- The right type of rod for the right type of lure.

Martha's Vineyard in the Spring and the Fall— especially with the marvelous Striped Bass and Bluefish Derby— is a fishing community.

Two years after using the old bamboo rods, we bought "new" fiberglass surf rods and green Penn 704 reels.

A few years later, the station wagon door came down on the rods and cracked them all.

A guy in a tackle shop on the Menemsha wharf encouraged us to build our own.

I did. Built two eleven-foot yellow Fenwick fiberglass rods.

We put the date on it and initialed it. 1976.

I see it every year because it is the only rod Ben uses fishing for blues.

Around 1980 an exciting new form of fiberglass came out called S glass. Brown like honey.

So, I built two eleven-footers.

Even though today's rods are made of much lighter, more advanced, and more sensitive graphite, I still fish with that same fiberglass rod I made over forty years ago. Brown S Glass.

Dad used to ask the questions he already knew the answers to—just to verify what he had heard from eight other guys. We got answers only because we never left the surf. We fished day and night, literally.

We fileted all our bluefish and smoked them when we got back home. It was the highlight of trip. Dad would wrap each smoked filet in wax paper, place it in a brown paper lunch bag, and take like two dozen of these bags to the Elks Club where he would doll them out to his closest friends in some clandestine way. With a nod or a head motion to this guy or that guy they would come out to the back of the place for his smoked fish. Don't tell anyone.

But no joke, guys waited all year for a piece of dad's smoked bluefish. And he took so much satisfaction providing it.

(However, the one year he wanted to cut off all the fish heads and take them all home for his Vietnamese and Filipino neighbors was a bridge too far for me. You know how hard it is to cut off fish heads?)

We saw surfcasting undergo a major change in the '90s because of three things:

1. SUVs became common. The "beach buggies" owned by surfcasters were now in everyone's driveway, providing the observing angler a way to now become an active surfcaster.
2. The fishing tackle industry improved with the explosion of more efficient line, lures, rods, and reels, increasing the new surfcaster's potential for success.
3. Training videos showed up on the internet. I know training might be too strong a word but it is true. Fishermen

new to surfcasting could access videos teaching them with a click everything it took the previous generation ten years to learn on the water's edge.

I have been so impressed with the new generation of surfcasters. They are young. They are friendly. They are kind. They are prepared. They are skilled. And they are willing to share information.

The epic Spring Runs on the Island are currently on the down cycle. Perhaps it will cycle back around in the future. Nevertheless, the Vineyard is a stellar spot to surf cast. The Spring surfcasting community is a welcoming one, and the intersection of water and land, dawn and dusk, stars and moon are beautiful.

It is also diverse. You can fish a real rip tide at Wasque, or a bathtub-like beach in Lobsterville. When certain fishing spots are negated by heavy wind, you can find another spot not impacted by that same wind.

Chappaquiddick's Wasque Rip.

Chappaquiddick's East Beach.

You can fish day and night. Both produce fish.

If you like camaraderie, there are always other fishermen out there willing to give you a basic and short summary of how they are doing. If you prefer to fish alone, you can spend hours without a conversation.

And because the Island has so many different spots, you can learn something new every year. This is a fact. The notes in my log identify something new I have learned every year.

And you can develop your own fishing pace and style.

For us it was this: If you come to a fishing community once a year for two weeks, you try NOT TO DO two things:

1. Try not to waste many tides fishing the wrong way or the wrong place.
2. Try not to sleep. You can do that all winter.

BEFRIENDING THE PLACE

"What are you guys gonna do with those?"
It is 1:00 a.m. on the beach at Wasque. We are filleting bluefish in the darkness on the back tailgate of the rusted-out red blazer.

One reason I am not a good bass fisherman after all these years is that for almost twelve years Dad and I did not fish for striped bass. There were years when the minimum size of a bass you could keep was thrity-six inches. Hard to catch bass that size unless you know the area really well.

Then there was a period of time when there was a moratorium on bass and you couldn't keep any.

When you are only coming for fourteen days, you have to be judicious about which species you want to target.

So, for many years we targeted bluefish only.

We only dreamed of the magnificent striped bass

Around 1976 I found Dad an ole Chevy Blazer which allowed us to drive on the beach. He was in heaven with that ole thing. He'd sweep it out with a little hand brush. He babied it even after you could see the highway through the rusted-out hole in the floorboard under your feet. He babied it even after the fabric on the ceiling sagged and the roof itself leaked. For this New York City bus driver, this ole Blazer was his chariot to the land of enchantment, on the water's edge, far from traffic and troubles. Foster Silva, the revered Chappy ranger, would let him park in the Cape Pogue Cedars at night and sleep in it when he got there a few days before our rental began.

When the old red Blazer finally gave out, he got another one just like it.

So here on the beach in the middle of a dark night around 1981, a curious fisherman has driven up from out of the darkness.

We had a nice little filet system set up on the tailgate of the Blazer. Side by side we filleted bluefish and stacked them in the cooler until we could put them on ice.

"Taking them back home to smoke. Guys love them."

"Then take mine, too." Said the stranger. "Anyone who loves bluefish enough to filet them out here this time of night can have mine, too."

That stranger was Ed Jerome. He had just settled on the Island. Ed went on to be a beloved principal in Edgartown, a leader in the fishing community who, with the help of a few others, brought new life to the Derby and the Island's fishing economy. He went on to be President of the Derby for years and a charter boat fisherman. He started a Derby-sponsored college scholarship program for Island high school students that still exists today.

Ed and I became friends over the years since we were both in education.

He taught me to drive the surf at night during high tide and to stop and cast whenever the headlights revealed tiny bait fish jumping out of the water near shore.

On May 31, 2011, according to my log, as we were driving by the Narrows of Pogue Pond and our headlights revealed that bait was jumping out of the water, I shared Ed's thirty-year-old advice with Ben.

"Then, let's do it," Ben said.

I stopped, let Ben out, turned off the engine, and grabbed the thermos for a cup of coffee. Before I could get the first sip, a bass on the end of Ben's line was walking him past my windshield and down the bank.

From that moment on, the Narrows has become a favorite night spot for Ben and me—and I think of Ed Jerome whenever I catch fish there.

Rest in Peace Ed, we are still doing it.

Eventually, we too sold our fish to the restaurants and market, especially Linda and Charlie Marinelli's farm/fish market. The Marinellis represented what was the heart of the Vineyard community in the late '70s and early '80s. Their small truck farm was primitive and active and successful. We used to arrive early in morning after a night of fishing and it was surreal. An agricultural oasis on an Island far away from the urban life we came from. Linda Marinelli later followed her passion into politics and served as an elected official on the Island for many years.

On one trip around 1982, the chef at the Colonial Inn in Edgartown told us he would buy five hundred pounds of bluefish filets that week. He stopped us after three days: we delivered 375 pounds of bluefish filets in three days. Three hundred and seventy-five pounds of *filets.*

None of the Island guys seemed to mind—I suspect because the overall size of our harvest was so small.

Massachusetts later required a legit commercial license. Dad bought a license and our "fish money" became coffee money, and gas money, and lure money, and hot breakfast at the Dock Street Café money. We had one rule: The fish money never left the Island. It always went back to the Island business owners. Still have that one rule.

I got a Massachusetts commercial rod and reel license when dad died twenty years ago and continue the tradition to this day. I think I am the last of that '70s and '80s Island group still selling bluefish.

I often think I should drop it. It might be politically incorrect.

But it seems to be a tangible link to my fishing roots and the Company I kept. It also resonates with that first moment I caught food from the ocean surf on our very first trip. The Net Result in Vineyard Haven sells out all the fresh bluefish I bring in. Consumers know the benefits of fresh, wild, hand-caught fish.

We all come to our annual vacations in different states of mind. Sometimes we are primed and pumped and full of anticipation. Other times we sleepwalk our tired selves to our vacation. For over twenty years I drove here from Omaha and back. Three years ago, an hour after beginning the twenty-four-hour drive from Omaha, I almost turned around and canceled. It had been a hard year and I was not ready to tackle all the tasks related to getting the gear safely across half the United States and prepping the rental house for the rest of the family that would be flying in later that week.

This year I find myself strangely unmoved. Happy to be going but not with the kind of excitement I feel most years. Not sure why.

My dad silently performed a gesture upon arriving every Spring. In my youthful impatience, I would hurriedly put on my waders, grab my rod, and run to the water's edge to make my long-awaited cast again. But this man who came over from Italy on a boat twice, fought hell on earth in the Pacific jungle battles of World War II, and drove a New York City bus the rest of his life, would walk out of the car and go straight to the surf, cupping his hands full of The Sea and washing his face with it. Cupping hands full of The Sea and pouring it over his head and neck, and finally rubbing his arms in The Sea.

We never spoke about it.

I used to think it was his way of greeting his good friend The Sea. A "So good to see you" kind of gesture.

He and The Sea would embrace and kiss each other on the cheek like two guys catching up with each other at a wedding.

I have come to do the same. I did not do it when I was young. Only after noticing how the Sea here had been not just a friend but Medicine. The kind of Medicine that has taken away anxiousness, sadness, fatigue. The kind of Medicine that has been restorative.

Finding Your Place is a wonderful gift. Befriending it takes time and work.

We have to open ourselves to the ecology of

the Place, *authentically* getting to know two or four people, customs, characteristics, expectations, rituals, and reasons.

It is one thing to Find Your Place, it is another thing to truly Befriend it.

Even though you could see the highway under the front seat of the Blazer we were thrilled. We now could drive to the water's edge to catch and clean our forty blues on the tailgate in 1976.

PART TWO
THIRTY STRAIGHT

WEEK ONE: MAY 18-24
TACKLE

"Hard enough to catch a bass. Now you want to make it even harder!"

This is the reaction I got from both Christin and Ben two months ago when I told them I spent the previous month prepping for the trip by replacing all the treble hooks on my bass lures with single inline hooks in order to reduce the chances of hurting fish to be released.

I respect the regal beauty and smarts of a striped bass so much that I want to give it as fair a chance as possible of winning the battle on the other end of my line. I remove the treble hooks and never have more than two single hooks on any bass lure.

I do not punish a hooked striper by having the drag on my reel set so loose that, while it extends the fight to the joy of the fisherman, it causes the fish to nearly die of exhaustion.

Surf fishermen have at least one "heavy rod" for casting two to four-ounce lures and a "light rod" for casting half to two-ounce lures and bucktails. Many fishermen have more than two. And a few fishermen have found a way to fish both heavy and light lures with the same rod.

My light rod had been a nine-foot graphite salmon rod which is the only rod I use for stripers. But over the last couple of years, I broke two handmade salmon rods at the ferrule joint while pulling a beached fish out of the wash. So, instead of building another salmon or steelhead rod, I will now try a nine-foot light surf rod I purchased at the tackle shop. It won't crack at the joint as easily as a salmon or steelhead rods.

It is my version of being a fly fisherman with spinning gear. Like a fly fisherman, I have stood next to guys who will catch four and five bass to my one because they are casting farther with their rod or they are using a lure larger than the one I can throw with my light set up.

I have come to terms with this over the years

because the feel of the strike and the weight of the fish on light tackle is the closest thing to feeling the animal with your hands as it battles in its own environment.

Besides, if it gives the bass a better chance of spitting the hook, I'm good with it.

For the last few years, Massachusetts has mandated that all bass under twenty-eight inches must be released. Should you land a keeper-size bass, you can only keep one a day. You cannot filet it where you catch it. It must be fileted in a more public locale.

Our family always places a piece of tape on our rods twenty-eight and a half inches from the butt of the rod. This becomes our ruler and a rule: You gently lay the fish on the sand and place the butt of the rod even with the tail of the fish. If the nose of the fish touches the tape when you measure it, you can keep it.

None of us have ever taken an undersized fish.
Ever.

Part of the fun and the challenge in any sport comes from playing by the rules of that sport. Right?

Ben releases most of his keepers.

But there was our infamous "tape night" on

Lobsterville Beach back on June 2 of 2010. At that time, Massachusetts regulations said each of us could catch two keepers a day. Here's the actual notation in my log:

> For The Record: In my 40 straight years, I have never seen this before. Christin, Ben, and I caught 13 keepers in 4 trips to Lobsterville and released at least 30-35 more bass most bout ½ inch short of the tape. Turns out the tape I put on our rods were all long. We probably caught 25 keepers.

When I discovered that the tape was at 29 inches and told the kids, they had a ball with very creative expressions of pain, lamenting how they would have been home sooner on those 4 nights. Somehow the amount of unnecessary pain and injury and fatigue and exhaustion and all manner of needless discomfort grew with each creative lament. I didn't know my kids could be so articulate.

Now, having just turned seventy and watching the rental prices of the Island skyrocket, I get the feeling that future trips are uncertain.

In memory of thirty days sleeping side by side with Dad in the station wagon fifty years ago, I concocted a plan: thirty straight nights and days with waders in the water.

But I have not told anyone about my plan.

Especially my wife, Catherine.

I took time at the end of every night—around 1:00 a.m.—to scribble down details from that day and night's fishing. These notes make up what follows. I have tried not to get bogged down in details. But I think I still did.

On the first of my thirty days, Christin arrives a few hours after I do. We stock the fridge and make the beds together. She decides to rest after a long day of travel so I run to Chappaquiddick so I can get my feet wet—boots wet—right away. It is always good to return to where you were when you last left. I discover it is the wrong time of the tide completely so I pivot to a spot called the Narrows where you can sometimes catch small stripers in the quiet calm waters of Pogue Pond.

The Chappy ferry, that little thing that carries three cars at a time on a four minute ride across the Edgartown harbor, stops running at 11:15 p.m. until Memorial Day weekend so I have one eye on the clock as I fish with the Narrows all to myself.

Not another person around. It is 10:30.

I hook a nice size striper and I giggle aloud as it fights.

I'm delighted to have a striper on again after a year away. First night!

First couple of hours! In the exact spot I dreamed about all Winter. How cool. Winter is over. I am back again!

It spits the hook just before I land it.

I smile and giggle in the dark.

I can't wait to tell Ben and Christin so they can once again rub it in. I enjoy the teasing they will send my way.

The very first bass of the trip spit the single hook that they both told me not to put on in the first place.

JIGGING

Leave me alone.
I am thick headed. Comfortable. Slow to change. Don't move the furniture. I like it this way.

It's a tradition. The first thing is to go buy ten to twelve Kastmasters at Coops Bait and Tackle to replenish what snapped off or got bitten off the year before. Coop once told me he tells customers that the bluefish don't arrive until this one guy shows up and buys a box of Kastmasters.

Writer and fisherman Nelson Sigelman is here this morning. When he finds out that Christin is in the car, he runs out to the parking lot to reconnect with her. Twenty years ago, in his book *Martha's Vineyard Outdoors,* he wrote a story about her catching a nice striper as a college freshman among a thick line of seasoned fishermen who shouted out and congratulated her as she walked by. The venerable Don Moore even kissed her on the cheek.

Nelson has not seen her since. He ushers her inside Coops and together they remember aloud that wonderful day.

He then announces, "Sometimes I am asked to read some of the stories aloud for a group here and there. The story of Christin is the one story I cannot read aloud. I cannot finish it. I always get choked up."

Nelson's sentiment reminds us that sometimes we underestimate the relationships developed through shared experiences with others during our annual vacations.

We grab his latest book off the shelf at Coops and ask him to sign it for us.

This trip we are staying in a cottage in Vineyard Haven, about a mile from Lake Tashmoo, a great fishing spot if you know where and how to fish it. I have never have fished it. Clueless.

But I know local legend Janet Messineo (*Casting into The Light*) fishes Tashmoo in the early Spring so I text Janet. She tells me to "Try fishing the Inlet."

Night two has me fishing in a spot I have never fished before. I text Ben in California who has been begging me for five years to explore more spots. He's delighted. Tashmoo is a really fishy place but I have no idea where to fish it. I set up inside the Inlet and try using a teaser which of course Ben has been urging me to do for five years. Yep.

I lament. Why can't I be left alone to fish my old-fashioned way in my old-fashioned places in my old-fashioned comfort zone?

No need to do new. I like things the way they are and have always been.

I am by myself at Tashmoo when a friendly young fisherman arrives and quickly introduces himself. After twenty minutes of fishing dusk nearby, Eric offers me one of his favorite lures before leaving. I decline but I am once again reminded of how this generation of fishermen is much more open, generous, and transparent than the old timers years ago.

I stay another hour but can't even get a hit. At

least I found out a bit more about the fabled Tashmoo and am secretly taking pride for having gone to a new spot—inching past my comfort zone.

Up until twelve years ago, fishermen on the Island did not regularly fish bucktails. Guys might have one somewhere among their lures but you never saw one—and for sure you never tied one on and fished with it.

A visiting fisherman from Connecticut named Billy Batterton changed all that. Billy simply showed up and caught bass all the time in front of all of us catching nothing. He caught bass after bass after bass for weeks after weeks while the rest of us got nada on our swimming lures.

Slowly a few fishermen tried it. Then a few more. All who tried it did better than those who did not. Within a few years everyone learned this new way of fishing. (It's actually a very old way of fishing that lost popularity and has now returned.)

Fishing a bucktail is different—and a bit more difficult—than fishing with a regular lure. You have to "jig it" upward occasionally as you reel it in.

How often do you jig it upward? Dunno.

How hard do you jig it upward? Dunno.

How deep do you try and let it sink before you start reeling it in? Dunno.

What's the speed of retrieve? Quickly, slowly, moderately? Dunno.

It can't be denied that jigging bucktails is more efficient and more effective catching bass in the surf at most places around the Vineyard. So now fishing a bucktail is something everyone does at times.

'Cept me and a few other old guys.

Billy taught his close friend Steph Pond and then he taught his friend Aaron. The three of them are elite bucktail fishermen. Elite. A word I rarely use.

Two years ago, Billy tutored our son Ben who, as Billy likes to say, "Has the gift." And indeed, Ben is one of those humanoids that has the gift of connecting with fish below the water and unseen.

But now add Ben to the number of guys calling me past my comfort zone and into this new way of fishing.

So, on my second full day of fishing, I run into Billy and Steph. Even though I haven't seen them in a year, the first thing Billy and Steph do is take me aside and tutor me. Billy and Steph are now making and selling their own bucktails through the Vineyard tackle shops. One of them pulls out a white bucktail and gives it to me. Insists on it. Gives one to Christin as well—despite the "Wait. No. I'll get one at Coop's. Please."

Billy reaches into his waders and produces the proper white tail to attach to the bucktail. Insists on it. Yeah, you have to have a tail, and it has to be a certain color.

What kind of tail? Dunno.

What color? Dunno.

But once again I am genuinely struck by their generosity and sincere interest in transferring knowledge. Perhaps I will catch more moments of generosity than fish during this thirty-day adventure.

I am feeling guilty.

Why is it that we can be so reluctant to move toward that which is more efficient, more productive?

What is it in our "tried and true" ways of working and playing and cooking and exercising and praying and venturing and abiding that we don't want to

explore,

upgrade,

expand,

improve,

enhance?

So, I awkwardly try to jig this stupid bucktail which I can't even feel on the end of my line and have no idea where it is or what it is supposed to do.

Naturally I catch nothing during the day or that evening. Take Christin home at dusk and return immediately to East Beach and fish in front of Dike's Bridge, one of my favorite spots and one rich in memory.

It is fishable. I switch back the lures I love love love fishing with.

But no fish.

I pull out in time to catch the Chappy Ferry before it stops at 11:15. Night Three is done.

Driving back to Chappy the next morning, Christin is studying the log and begins to giggle and giggle and then reads aloud:

May 20, 2010: Billy the Jigger and Steph the chef try to give Dad a jig.

Steph tells Dad "Stay with it, in four years or so you will have it down.

It will be the best thing you've ever done fishing-wise."

"DAD! THAT WAS TWELVE YEARS AGO TODAY! Twelve years ago to this *very day*! They HAVE BEEN TRYING TO GET YOU TO JIG FOR TWELVE years MAN. TWELVE years! Are you stubborn or what?"

We laughed out loud for five minutes.

"Read it again, Christin, read it for me again."

After more laughter I agree to begin jigging if she would do the same. She agrees.

I told Billy and Steph what Christin had discovered from twelve years ago.

Big grins and chuckles.

But no fish. Nothing but mop like weeds.

On Night Four I was hoping on fishing in front of the Dikes' Bridge again until the last Chappy Ferry, but the wind came up choppy again so I got out of the wind and fished the Narrows alone. This is one of the gifts of the Vineyard. When the wind is bad in one spot you can move to a spot more favorable to that wind.

Caught seven bass, each about two inches short. Delightful and fun.

Christin is always the first person in our

family to catch a keeper. She always catches it during the day. Not the night. On day five she does it again.

But this time it was a little different. For the first time ever, she caught it on a bucktail.

The one Steph Pond gave her.

Christin and one of her annual day time stripers. May 2003.

SHORE BIRDS

I come for the birds. With all my heart, I come for the birds. When they leave, the whole fishing experience *completely* changes and something is lost.

Piping plovers shut down most of Chappaquiddick beginning around Memorial Day at the end of May. Fishermen and their families have shortened their stay or stopped coming all together due to the impact these birds have on access. The debate over being protective without be excessively restrictive is a real issue on Chappy.

But these are not the shore birds that matter the most to me. The shore birds I come to Island to see over and over again consists of a flock of fishermen who migrate from all over the U.S.A. to gather on the shores of Chappy for two or three weeks every Spring at this time.

We wait all year to see these birds. They have been landing here at the end of every spring for the last thirty to forty years.

We wonder every winter if we will see them again come Spring.

All these birds can really, really catch fish:

Polly Alden

Best buds P.J. Carr and Joe Cefalo from Boston.

Bill Ricci from Florida.

The trio of Dave Kasoff, Sid Siegel, and Larry Bressler, who drive from Philly and Florida.

Joe and Jan Bals who drive from Florida.

Phil Bibeau from New Hampshire with his sweet dog Piper who replaced his previous dog Leland.

Lance and Lois Dimock from Connecticut.

Billy Batterton, his father in law Bill Moe, and their friend Aaron Hurley—also from Connecticut.

Jake Rudy and his grandsons Jeffrey and Peter from Pennsylvania.

Jim Olsen who drives all the way from Washington State.

Joe Dart and his wife come from Western Massachusetts.

There are also several new birds arriving every spring but it is these veteran birds that make up a community wherein everyone knows each other's stories, plans, and health status.

With little or no communication during the year, this reliable and remarkable collection of characters land on the beach around the second or third week in May. Like birds returning after the winter.

Every year.

You never see these birds anywhere except in the sands of Chappy.

Christin, Ben, and I are honored to Keep Company with these characters. They all have their own stories and could write their own books.

For sure. One hundred percent.

Sid is ninety-five. From Florida, he drives a couple of hours to put his car on the Amtrak auto train. He gets off in Virginia and drives a few more hours to Philly to catch up with Dave and

Larry. Dave is ninety. Larry, the young pup, is seventy-two. These three birds come as one.

Sid loves to show off his full head of hair. When my wife caught up with these three guys on the beach this year, Sid immediately changed to one of his favorite hats. The one with the logo "Fish Fear Me. Women Want Me."

Joe Cefalo and P.J. insist that it is the other way around.

In their prime, David and Sid took on the challenge of surf fishing the Outer Banks of North Carolina around Hatteras. Surf fishing at Hatteras used to be epic, they say. Sid once landed a fifty pound red drum there. It was at the Outer Banks where they met Joe Cefalo, P.J., and Bill Ricci. One thing led to another and they all decided to come fish the Vineyard where they arrive like migrating birds every May.

These days, David cares more about the cooking then the catching—although he cares a lot about that as well. The dinner menu every night reads like Michelin. Larry lamented that David was upset with him because he forgot to bring the *wooden* salad bowl needed to properly crush/mix the Caesar's. How could you forget the *wooden* bowl? How can I make a proper Caesar's without one?

They kept driving an ancient Jeep Wagoneer—the one with wooden side panels—up here until just two years ago.

Larry came here inexperienced but now has it figured out. It has been so much fun watching Larry put in hours and hours in the surf year after year to get better and better at it. I have fished next to him and watched him catch fish I could not.

And oh yeah, in 2003, Sid, David, and Larry took the hooks off their lures because they "got tired of bringing in the big ones."

P.J. and Joe are seriously good fishermen and have made it their mission to keep an eye on the trio of birds Dave, Sid, and Larry. They both retired in 1992. Each bought a Jeep and fished for four months starting on the Vineyard and ending in Hatteras. Prior to that they fished Hatteras for ten years, where they first met some of the other Shore Birds.

P.J. recently told me this story: "In May one year, Joe Cefalo and I were leaving the beach to go back to the house. We met Bill Batterton and his father-in-law Bill Moe at Arruda's (a spot on Chappy). It was loaded with sand eels so we decided to stick around. From 5:00 to 9:00 p.m. we caught a few bluefish way out. Around 9:00 p.m. when it got dark, the stripers arrived. The four of us spread out and fished hard til 2:00 a.m. We stopped only because we were beat. All stripers were over thirty inches and fat. A lot of them were thirty-six to forty-nine inches. On the way out, Bill Moe said 'Wait a minute, I need one more for fifty.' Joe, Bill, and I looked at each other and said: 'If he has fifty, we all must have had fifty.' That means that on that great night we four caught and released close to two hundred big stripers. What a memory."

Lance from Connecticut gained fame for a giant striper he caught several years ago and fishes all day long. Lois, a retired early childhood specialist, is known for her embroidery and the wonderful baked breads and cookies that magically appear out the back of their truck. They and their dogs fish at their own pace and always seem to be around the fish. They would do anything for you if you needed help.

Polly has been fishing Chappy for thirty-seven years. She and her husband Dick were Shore Birds early. And Polly continued after his untimely passing. The rest of the birds were there for her every time she returned.

She fishes mostly by herself, eight hours a day. Has her favorite spots but always seems to set aside time for lunch rendezvous somewhere with Lance and Lois. Polly is one of the few Shore birds that keep bluefish. She takes meticulous care of the fish she catches. Watching the reverent and careful way she cleans her catch is something I will never forget. I love the way she fishes and I have told her so.

She told me, "After my husband passed away, my fishing buddies asked me if I would still come down to Chappy. Without hesitation I said absolutely. M.V. has always been one of my 'safe places.' Although it may not be as safe now, I still feel safe on Chappy, mainly because of the great people I've met here over the years. I don't do much night fishing anymore because lots of people I know don't come out for night fishing and may not be able to help me if I need it. Plus, I don't like running into skunks!"

Phil parks his truck in the same spot every day, pulls out his chair, lets Piper run on a leash and waits for the fish to show up. No one is more relaxed than Phil. He has been doing it this way for years. And Piper the Dog might be the most popular Shore Bird of all. It is quite a sight to see unshaven grown men in their waders lying in the sand playing and giggling with this cute little dog.

Phil used to always fish with Gary Tyson before he got sick and passed away. Gary holds a special spot in our memory box. Around fifteen years ago, he told Christin and I not to leave him one night. He assured us things would pick up in thirty minutes. Sure enough, the bass showed up right there and it has been our favorite night spot ever since: Chappy's East Beach right in front of Dike's Bridge.

I still giggle at the time Gary and his wife were fishing there with us in a rainstorm. She is watching a movie in the car on the new-fangled TV screen on the dashboard. Gary, fighting heavy rain and surf, brings in a striper. Walks it quickly to the car to show his wife. She rolls down the window in the rain and tells him she likes to cook the smaller ones. Go get a different one.

He ended up bringing her like 5 in the rain that night until she decided which size would do just fine.

She finished the movie too.

Jake, eighty-two, brings his grandsons Jeffrey

and Peter with him every year and they quietly go to their favorite places and catch more fish than the rest of us. They fish day and night. Jake used to come with his beloved brother Joe before Joe passed away. Told me, "My favorite memories of Chappy are the times I spent with family. First my wife who has accompanied me on every trip, the time spent on the beach with my brother until his death, and the introduction of my grandsons to the area. But it is also the friendships we have developed here. My grandsons and I often speak of those acquaintances and the help so many have provided to us."

Joe Dart has been coming maybe fifty years himself. He was one of the first to exchange his surf rod for a saltwater fly rod which he uses exclusively these days. Told me last year that the increased restrictions on beach access because of the protected birds along with the rising costs of a rental house were making it harder and harder to justify the trip. He's practically a local up here. So well respected.

"Washington Jim" Olsen is known for the way he fishes rubber shads and broken back Sebiles. He always gets more fish than the rest of us. Whenever I fish next to him I go to school. Like

Ben, he has the uncanny ability to tell what is going on in the water after a few minutes of casting. Can tell you where the fish are, what the contour of the ocean bottom is like, etc. He also has multiple degrees in the natural sciences. One night a few years ago we were fishing Lobsterville together and I looked up at the magnificent star-filled sky and said:

"Jim, look at how many moving stars are out tonight! Look! See that one moving left to right? Crazy right? How cool is that?"

"Those are satellites."

"Oh. Well, they must have some serious lights on them if we can see them from here. Right?"

"They are reflecting off the sun."

"Oh."

Ninety-year-old Joe and Jan drive up from Florida and fish really hard. Have been doing so forever. Dawn to dusk. Often you would see Joe out alone with Jan in the car. Sometimes they would cast together. Sometimes they'd sit in the car together where Jan would read while Joe napped behind the steering wheel. He was a bona fide fisherman, much like his good fishing buddies Joe and P.J. Back home in Florida he manages the local St. Vincent DePaul center serving those in need of food, clothes, and a place to stay. A noble man of quiet grace. The Bals missed this trip. Joe's health had been declining.

All these Shore Birds are gentle and caring and funny and focused. There is no rowdy partying or loud bravado. No foul language. They are all straight up solid surfcasters.

"See you next year" gets harder and harder to say the older we get. We look into each other's eyes a few seconds longer now. Made it a point to spend a squish more time with Sid this trip. When it was finally time for the three amigos to leave, I draped my arm around him and told him how much we loved being with him.

He chose to say goodbye like this:

"My dad came from a poor Jewish family. He sold newspapers and had no education. As I was ready to leave home, he said to me 'I can't give you any help because I don't have any money. And I can't advise you much because I don't have an education. But I can tell you what is the most important thing to remember: Be A Good Person.' So, I think I've done that. I tried to be a good person. Never made enemies. I think I was a good person."

Then, with a smile and a chuckle he said, "Wasn't hard!"

Lois Dimock with a blue from the Cape Pogue Gut.

A few Shore Birds: Larry Bressler, myself, David Kasoff, PJ Carr, Sid Siegel, and Joe Cefalo. Two of us are in our 70s, two in their 80s, and two in their 90s.

Joe Bals with a beautiful keeper.

Aaron Hurley with a blue from Pogue Pond.

Billy Batterton and his dad Bill, whom Billy says is the reason he first came here.

Lance Dimock and his 50 lb bass early evening July 13, 1987.

RUIN THINGS

"CAST TO THE LEFT!" he screamed at me at the top of his voice.

There is a rhythm and cadence to surfcasting side by side and most of the time everyone can fish without hooking up with others. You get crossed if you cast in the wrong direction. You also get crossed if one person throws longer than the person next to him and reels it in at a different speed. The longer cast stays in the tide longer and can carry your lure right in front of the person casting and retrieving his lure down tide next to you.

On my last day of fishing *last year*, a beautiful afternoon with bluefish present, I found myself fishing side by side with Steph Pond and another local fisherman. Our lines crossed as they sometimes do.

This guy turned and screamed at me to cast to his left as if I was a rookie who just arrived.

I remember when this man first came to the Island. He was brash and loud at first but he developed into a valuable member of the Island community.

He knew me as a fisherman.

When he went off on me, I took it personally.

It was disrespectful.

Crestfallen, I pulled my line up out of the water and drove away.

I noticed that his wife, who had seen and heard the whole thing, got out of her chair to scold the guy.

When I arrived to the other spot down the beach, guys noticed that there was something wrong and asked why my shoulders were slumped.

"You just left here. Why are you back so soon? What happened up there?"

"Guy just yelled at me and told me how to cast."

"Whaaat?" "Don't let it bother you." "Who was it?"

"Doesn't matter."

But it did. I could not get past it all winter. I made up my mind I would express myself the next time I saw him.

So, on day six of the first week, when Christin left the surf to go back to the car for a coffee break, I approached him.

"If you ever tell me how to cast again, I will throw your stuff in the ocean."

He knew exactly what I was referring to and began to blame me for crowding him last year—something I was taught to never do.

We yelled profanities at each other back and forth for thirty seconds.

Then I walked away.

A few minutes later, he re-engaged, yelling at me from down the beach. I walked back to confront him. Unfortunately, Christin was returning back from the car just as things were heating up again between him and me.

She jumped between us yelling, "Walk Away! Walk Away!"

We eventually did.

In the months afterwards, in the quiet of my normal life, I wondered:

Why had I harbored my hurt for a year? Why did I gush a profanity as soon as he made excuses?

I think I may have figured it out.

Over the last two or three years, as I have moved closer to seventy, I have detected more dismissal in the interactions I have had with the public—be it the mechanic or the new accountant or the store owner or the builder.

The occasional dismissal is a new thing. Didn't hear it before but now I do. I assume it has to do with being perceived as old.

And it stings.

It was the sting of his instructions that hurt me.

He knew me. He knew of the years I had been doing this.

Still, he felt I needed to be instructed.

I told him he had issues.

So do I.

Don't we all.

But what I remember most is the way this polluted the beach. The giggle and enthusiasm and camaraderie among all the fishermen before the beef was replaced by this strange SILENCE.

It was not the same silence found in the cast. This was silence that chased enthusiastic chatter.

The silence was not a pleasant one. It was a dead silence. Or a dread silence.

It was followed by fishermen pulling their lines out and heading back to their cars.

Eventually it was just Steph Pond and I. Until he too left in dead silence.

A communal place of grace was polluted by dis-grace generated by two knuckleheads.

I fished the empty space by myself.

Fifty-one Spring runs on the Island and I had never had a beef with anyone.

This was me making the decision to stand up for myself.

I do not regret one inch of it. In fact, I wish I had been more forceful.

But it ruined a good time being had by all.

And Christin had never seen this from her father.

LOG DAY

Betting on history.

The Zane brothers were awesome fishermen. They were Shore Birds for twenty years until they stopped coming about ten years ago.

Could they fish! They always found the fish and reached them with football field long casts. Dave, Rick, and Rob, and their mom, dad, uncles, and nephews are still missed even today.

My log for May 24, 2009 reads:

Wrong turn over Dike's Bridge. Rick, Rob, and Dave Zane go toward Pond.

I see them go by but I turn right and go towards East Beach.

> The Zanes got 40 blues 2 hours after high tide at the Cedars.
> I missed it.

From that year on, I have always fished the Pogue Pond Cedars on May 24.

Two years later, my log for May 24, 2011:

> Blues show up at Cedars fourth year in a row on this date.
> 2 hr. before high tide. Key seems to be SW wind.
> Dave and Rick Zane got about 30 blues. I got 12.

Two years later, May 24, 2013 reads:

> Aaron (our oldest son) Christin and I catch fish in the Pond on top in front of Cedars.
> Just before high tide. SW Wind.

May 24 is now my "Log Day" during which I make it a priority to fish in front of the Cedars on the shore of Pogue Pond on Chappy. The blues are not in the Chappy surf every year at this time, but if they are around, I believe they will show up here by May 24.

Today is my seventh day in the water and I will spend a chunk of it here with Christin. She and I remind ourselves of the time the high tide covered the road out and prevented us from leaving. But it also prevented anyone else from approaching. Locked in on both sides, and thus isolated from everyone and anyone, we caught bluefish upon bluefish for two hours.

Today, we fish a few times during the day on both sides of high tide but there are no fish.

I return alone at Dusk and I am feeling sentimental. Always do here at The Pond, as we call it.

For old time's sake, I put on an orange Spofford ballistic.

Al Spofford was legendary for his ability to fish and make innovative lures for the rest of the fishing community back in the '70s, '80s, and '90s. He was part of the group that helped upgrade the Martha's Vineyard Striped Bass and Bluefish Derby and is the M.V. Derby Hall of Fame.

I consider Spoffy to be one of my teachers. As a young man in my twenties I hounded him. I asked him every possible question I could about the best time of the tide to fish The Pond, and then The Rip. I asked him what wind direction was most favorable, what speed of retrieve was best for what lures (especially the metal Kastmaster, my favorite).

I asked him why he placed the first guide of his rod a certain distance from the reel, and toward the end I even asked him about the latest lure he was developing, which was CIA-level secret.

He was annoyed with me at first but I think he warmed up to me after a few years due to the fact that Dad and I stuck with it.

Spoffy took me under his wing before it was over, not something he did with a lot of fishermen other than his buddies Don Mohr, Gordon Ditchfield, and Arthur "Flash" Winters.

There were so many other Island fishermen in the '90s that I only heard about. Porky Francis, Karen Kukolich, Steve and Ed Amaral. There was Dan Purdy, one of the early saltwater fly fishermen, the passionate Roberto Germani whom I had seen fish from an inner tube, a raft and whatever else he could float on. He was among the first of the old timers to Catch and Release.

Bob and Fran Clay have been fishing Chappy

for years. Fran tells me there is nothing like catching false albacore here in the pond during the Fall Derby.

Then there was Peter Johnson who made the Robert lures. It was a treat to fish next to him and hear him describe the aerodynamics of surf casting. He insisted that you get much better action on your plug if you *don't* stand in the water. He insisted that you stand up on the beach because being above water level was key to getting the most action out of your lure. Has all to do with the billowing of the line coming off your rod and down toward the lure.

Many times, as I fished the Pond next to Spoffy, he would always remind me to bang the top of the water with my lure when it landed to "See if we can raise a blue here, me and you."

So at dusk today, my memory has me fishing with him again. As the sun sets in my face I counted back to the old timers and the years of discovery for us: the signs of fish in this Pond and the various ways to work for them.

After casting deep down memory lane for thirty minutes, a fish took a swipe at Spoffy's orange popper just before I pulled it out of the water. Like the guy in Jaws who looked wide-eyed after seeing the Shark, I too woke out of my haze and realized the familiar sign of a bluefish. On alert now, I concentrated on the speed and action of my retrieve on the next two casts. Spoffy always said not too fast and not too slow.

The bluefish hit, and as I landed it I was well aware of the irony, catching it on an old-time Spoffy ballistic missel in his honor, in the middle of reliving experiences of fishing with him and the other old timers here in this place twenty-five to thirty years ago.

On the way back to Dike's Bridge I stopped off at East Beach and fished the surf for stripers in what is usually calm water. Caught a nice striper that just "made the tape" on my rod (twenty-eight-inch keeper) but I released it.

Fileted the bluefish at Dikes and froze it as soon as I got home.

I'll eat it in their honor this fall.

First week has ended.

May 24 had produced again, don't you know.

Bluefish on in the Cape Pogue Pond.

Christin with a blue caught on Peter Johnson's Roberts lure, her favorite.

WEEK TWO: MAY 25-31
COMFORT ZONE

What was THAT? I asked myself.

I had been thinking about eighty-two-year-old Jake Rudy from Pennsylvania who used to come with his beloved and departed brother Joe and now brings his grandsons, Jeremy and Peter. Together they quietly and inconspicuously fish in their favorite spots, casting their favorite lures regardless of what all the other fishermen are doing. And they catch fish.

Maybe I should be more like Jake.

For years I have dreamed of being more like Jim Mullins, one of the local fishermen I admire most. He fishes alone most of the time, in spots he has found to be productive over time, with lures he has confidence in, regardless of what all the others are doing.

Many nights, fishing alone in the dark on Chappy, I will notice near or far one solitary light from a Jeep down the beach doing the same thing. Jim Mullins by himself.

Week One was really difficult. I had tried jigging a bucktail for five hours a night for five nights and was miserable. The weeds were so thick that you would have twenty seconds of clear water on each cast before getting bogged down with a mop full of weeds. I pulled out one fish in ten hours of fishing, which is okay most of the time but not when you have to stop after every cast to de-weed your line and your lure.

I saw some big keepers caught last week but I was still trying to figure out the whole bucktail thing and was seriously questioning why I was fishing in this new and difficult way instead of the comfortable way I have come to love over the years.

Maybe I should choose to fish the way I enjoy even if it won't be the most productive.

Maybe I should fish the way I am most comfortable even if it might not be the most efficient.

Maybe this is the big decision I must come to terms with moving forward.

I begin my second week by returning to the Pond for more bluefish. I go with the Spoffy orange lure again and fish hard for an hour and a half with no luck.

Yesterday was the day of Tribute. Yesterday was the Gift Bluefish. Yesterday was Fish with Spoffy Day. Log Day.

Not today.

I move on to fish for bass in the Narrows of the Pond as dusk moved into dark.

Get eight bass on my trusty Yozuri darter. Each one just an inch or two short of a keeper.

I am the only one around and the hour and a half was just like I remembered it all winter.

Best of all, I am using my favorite lure in a place and manner I enjoy most.

On the way toward the Chappy ferry I decide to stop at my favorite spot on East Beach.

On my first cast I felt a slight bump in the wash just before pulling the lure out of the water. The same thing happened on my second cast: a slight hit in "the wash" where the white of the wave washes up into the shore.

It is pitch dark. Can't see the lure in front of me. So what was that?

I remembered something Ben and Washington Jim both told me: sometimes it is best to cast down the beach line instead of straight out because your lure will spend more time in the wash, should the bass be there.

As soon as I did, I hooked up with a keeper bass.

First keeper striper of the trip!

Forget the whole bucktail jigging thing. Got this one fishing my way! On my favorite lure in my favorite place.

We got this Jake. We got this Jim. I see you.

Jake Rudy with Jeffrey and Peter.

Jake Rudy with Jeffrey.

THE TUG

The next day I am reminded of what has motivated me most over the years:
The tug of a bluefish.
When I have struggled at times to get to the Vineyard due to deaths, pressing work issues, raising a young family, driving halfway across America, bills, etc., it was recalling the magic of The Tug that always helped me do the work of coming here.
The tight pounding and pulsating pull of a bluefish is unique and exhilarating. This Tug is a completely honest connection between you and a very powerful fish fighting for its life.
From the first bluefish I caught in 1971 and

every one since I have found this truth: Time Stands Still with The Tug.

Time.

Stands.

Still.

Many fishing magazines refer to the bluefish as the best fighting fish in the ocean, pound per pound. At Wasque, there is nothing like trying to pull in a six to eight pound bluefish against the rip tide.

Most of the fishermen on the Island have told me that bluefish are the reason they got hooked on surfcasting.

And nowadays almost everyone releases every bluefish back to the sea after The Tug.

Blues made their first appearance on Days Eight and Nine of this trip.

It was just Christin and me at The Rip in the fog and rain when they arrived. The Tug was back and we loved it. So cool.

We got six on both days.

Took them to the market where Mike Holtham at The Net Result began my tab. These early fish were bigger than normal, averaging six pounds per fish gutted.

That evening I made the forty minute drive up

Island to Lobsterville, a place I dream of all winter. The water at Lobsterville is usually very soft and the bass always show up there at some point every Spring to the delight of fly fishermen mostly.

The sun sets in your face there and the stars there fill the night sky like LEDs.

I usually make this trip on my first or second night every year but Christin has been reminding me that our log repeatedly notes that we never catch fish there until later in May. So I have resisted going up to Lobsterville for seven or eight nights now and have focused more on Chappy.

Fished Lobsterville two and a half hours without a hit. Then around 10:30 I switched to a reliable old green wooden Boone needle fish that had been successful the last few years. I had been deliberately waiting till deep darkness to throw it. On the first cast, I caught my second keeper bass of the trip.

An inch bigger than the minimum.

Turned out to be the only fish I would have for the rest of Week Two.

Blues disappeared after their two-day visit. They usually do and then return four or five days later.

Went back to Lobsterville the next night and caught four smaller bass in a twenty minute bite but that was it.

At dusk on night thirteen, the end of Week Two, I fished an undeveloped place up Island that I have had my eye on for a year. But I discovered that it is really unfishable.

Eight ticks crawled on the front of my waders in the time it took to walk to the spot through tall grass.

After getting to the spot, I discover that the rocky bottom prohibits my walking in the water to the place I want to be. I end up fishing under trees close to shore.

When I return, there are ticks on my car windows as well as two inside on the dashboard.

It is not quite dark, so I decide to race forty minutes to the Chappy Ferry and try to get another two hours of fishing there since today is the first day that the Chappy Ferry runs on its summer schedule. The last boat will be at midnight instead of 11:15.

One pays attention to such details. It makes the night last longer.

I returned to the Narrows of Pogue Pond on Chappy and caught one bass after what seemed a very empty week. But here's the thing: after releasing that one fish back to the Pond, in the quiet of the night, I noticed how fast my heart was beating.

And I loved it.

I had spent Memorial Day on the water with my wife, Catherine, and Christin, hanging out with the Shore Birds, some of whom I may never see again.

Aside from The Tug of the Bluefish and the Pull of the Bass, there is the Bond of Friendship.

Reconnecting with this annual community of good people makes the trip so wonderful and delightful and decent and keeps us all.

Coming back.

Ben , Christin, and The Tug.

THE CAR

"I am a PROFESSIONAL."

I say that just to start stuff with the kids. Always elicits a roll of the eyes or a dry "Yeah okay" as we make our way around in The Car.

While other fishermen have "the boat," the surfcaster has "the car."

Like a boat, they use the car to get to the fish.

Like a boat, they use a car to carry everything they need to do the fishing. It may look a bit chaotic inside once in a while (often) but the surfcaster knows exactly where every little thing is. You will never see a surfcaster fumbling in their car mumbling, "Where did I put it?"

The car faithfully takes you out over all kinds

of terrain. All kinds of weather. All kinds of hours. Then it faithfully brings you home late at night and sits outside reliably there for you when you are ready again.

How can a surf fisherman not have a fondness and a relationship with The Car?

In our family, the kids have made The Car a very special space. We share this space on the way to here and there. We sit side by side here in the middle of the night, often cold, sharing a thermos of coffee at 2:00 a.m., wet and exhausted.

Sometimes during the day the cooler in the back of the Car is filled with our catch. Most of the time it is empty.

There is a transparency and intimacy about this space. And it is as friendly and as safe as any other space in our lives.

In this space, the kids debate social issues of the day, like the use of gender specific pronouns to go along with one's name, or the merits/concerns associated with universal health care.

One year I heard one of them tell the other, "I have issues with your Point of View"

The other responded, "I have issues with your issues."

All manner of discussion from the high level complicated to the mundane come from humans sitting in The Car while wearing chest high waders surrounded by tackle boxes, coolers, and yesterday's sandwich bags. And oh yeah, it smells of fish.

Catherine, my wife, won't enter The Car without the can of Febreze.

The Car also seems to be the space where the kids get to tell Dad something important they have been mulling over for months or the many questions they seek to answer for themselves related to the direction and content of their lives.

And it works both ways. My kids don't like to call shotgun because they know whoever sits next to driver gets peppered with questions, observations, and a random and steady stream of consciousness. With an occasional tap on the arm to affirm a thought.

"Stop hitting me!" happens a lot.

Yesterday it was, "Good luck mom. He talks NON STOP to whoever sits in the front seat. But it's okay. If you don't say anything, he'll answer his own questions. Has a conversation with himself."

The Car is the space where Dad gets to ask his kids stuff he wants to know about their lives.

A few years ago, I asked Christin, sitting quietly in the passenger seat, what she, a young college professor about to pursue tenure at the time, saw as her trajectory.

"TRAJECTORY? TRAJECTORY? It's 1:30 at night and we have been fishing since six o'clock and you want to know about my TRAJECTORY? My only trajectory is to get to bed! Maybe a trajectory to get a shower!

"TRAJECTORY? It's nearly two in the morning! Go away. Go away with your trajectory!"

We laughed about that all winter.

I asked her again a year later on the card I sent her for her birthday.

The best part is the abundance of good-natured teasing tossed around in this Car.

To stir up some stuff, I occasionally point out examples of my prowess.

"You know I can tell how much coffee to pour into the thermos, when to stop, and how much room to leave for cream. You know I can do that without looking into the thermos, right? Don't need to look into the thermos or get no flashlight on it. Coffee and cream comes out perfect every time. I can tell when to stop pouring in the coffee by the sound, and the feel.

You know why? Cause I am a PROFESSIONAL."

"Your mother tried to buy me new binoculars. But why? See these here binoculars" (pulled from under the driver's seat) Forty-five years old. Grandpa's binoculars. But now they are monoculars. If you close one eye you can see just fine.

"Monoculars. You just have to know how to work them. See me? I know how to work 'em. I don't need no new binoculars. Why not? Because I'm a PROFESSIONAL."

At the end of the second week of this trip—when the fishing was really hard and non-productive—I went fishing to a new underdeveloped spot on the North Shore that was not scheduled to be open to the public until Fall.

I waded thru brush and into the water at dusk that night but it was rocky and I couldn't traverse the rocks in the water without losing my balance. So I fished right there in front of the brush. The wind was strong and my first cast got blown into the trees. Hung my favorite Yozuri mag darter in the trees and lost it. Had to cut the line.

Re-tied another lure and next cast same thing.

Hung it up in the same tree. (At least I was able to pull this one free).

Pulled out after about an hour since I couldn't wade around the corner and fish like I wanted to.

Looked at the clock and figured I still had time to run out to Chappy, forty-five minutes away.

I fished Chappy from 8-10:45 p.m. Long enough and dark enough to be worthwhile.

Coming home from East Beach on Chappy, I heard bass slapping under the Dikes' Bridge around 11:00 p.m. The last Chappy ferry boat was now running at midnight, so I stopped to make a few casts. I never actually fish the water under the bridge itself so it was kinda new to me.

Hooked the bridge.

Had to walk out of the water and up the bridge, reeling in line as I walked until finally finding my lure and unhooking it from the wood.

Returned to my spot in the water and did the exact same thing again on the next cast.

Hooked the bridge.

Once I unhooked it, I returned to the water, made a few more clean casts, had a few hits, but had lost so much time hooking and unhooking Dikes Bridge that I had to pull out in order to catch the last ferry. Made it with five minutes to spare.

I shared all this with Christin in the front seat of the Car as we went back out the next morning.

"So you hooked a tree twice and then you hooked a bridge twice. Is that what you're telling me?"

"Yeah."

"You know why you did that?" she giggled.

"Cause I haven't slept in like a year."

"Nope. Cause you are a PROFESSIONAL."

Our traditional cup of coffee after cleaning fish and getting them on ice packs in the cooler.

THIS HUMBLES YOU

"Going fishing for a few weeks."

"Have a nice time. That'll be relaxing."

Fishing brings to mind a casual sport. Throw a line in the water. Put your feet up. Eat something out of the cooler. Chat with a close friend. Enjoy the sunshine. Retreat. And maybe catch something.

Not with Surfcasting.

You are completely at the mercy of Mother Nature and the Fish.

She has to let you in the door.

Then the Fish have to invite you to stay.

You can plan a night or a day of fishing, postpone other things you could do with that time, prepare and organize your gear, and do whatever is required to make the trip to the fishing spot only to find out that Mother nature is not open to your visit.

The wind is blowing way too strong the wrong way.

The time of the tide is nonproductive.

The water is so full of weeds that you can't cast and retrieve.

Even if the fish are there and even if they would invite you to stay, you can't contact them unless Mother Nature opens the door.

The flip is also true. Maybe Mother Nature is open to your visit: the wind speed and direction is fine, the water is not weedy, and the time of tide is exactly what you hoped for—but the Fish don't invite you to stay. They are not biting. Sometimes, despite Mother's nature's welcoming you, they are not even home.

And then there are the times when Mother Nature lets you in and the fish ARE home—you can see them and hear them and feel them and even sometimes smell them—but they are not feeding right now, *thank you very much.*

We can't control any of this. That's why surfcasting humbles you.

Repeat: Prepare well and come correct.

But Mother Nature has to be open to your visit and The Fish have to invite you to stay.

I have found this to be comforting as I get older. Cathy will ask "How long will you be gone tonight?"

More and more I reply, "Depends on whether the fish invite me to stay."

Most of Week Two was another painful grind through weeds thick as red carpet and wind that prevents you from casting. It was practically impossible to make contact with fish—if they were even there.

When I say grind I mean grind. You could only cast your lure out a third as far as usual due to the wind blowing it back toward you. You crank it ten seconds before it is bogged down in seaweed which you have to strain to reel in so you can cast again.

With the same result.

Cast after cast like this.

For hours.

For several nights and days in Week Two my arms and hands ached from the strain of pulling in weeds. On a couple of back-to-back nights I pulled out my line after a few hours shift in the water and made it home by 11:00 p.m., just in time to see who won the Celtics game. (They were in the finals against the Warriors.) Most of these nights and days the locals did not even venture out, so I found myself fishing alone; me and the dang weeds.

That's why surf fishing is not the kind of thing conjured up by, "Going fishing? Have a nice time."

Tide matters as well.

It works like this:

- Figure out what part of the tide the fish seem to bite.
- Figure out what time of the day that will be.
- As you plan the next few days ahead, remember that the tide begins forty-five to fifty minutes later every day.

Islander Ralph Peckham and 17 lb. 2022 Derby blue caught on his On Again metal lure.

For the last three nights, the striper bite seemed to be the first two hours of the Incoming tide. In other words, two hours after low tide.

So, if on Saturday low tide is three in the afternoon, the bite might pick up around five that evening. Got it?

But stripers traditionally seem to be more active at night then they are during the day. (Not everyone agrees about this.) So, on our hypothetical Saturday, you might have the right time of the tide but it's the wrong part of the day. It might be too early in the day. Too much sunlight? Water too warm?

Now, try to forecast what it looks like on, say, the upcoming Thursday. Ready?

Low tide will be around 6:30 p.m. Add two hours and the hypothetical bite might start around 8:30 p.m. Dusk. That's much, much better.

Identify what you think is the sweet spot in the tide then see if it matches up to a sweet time of day.

Often we will look at several spots around the Island to see which spot might have the most favorable combination of Tide and Time of Day over the next two or three days.

But you also have to factor in the Wind. I personally think the direction of the wind is not as important as so many surf fisherman seem to think. To me it's not so much about the direction as it is the velocity. A Northeast wind is usually not a good thing on Chappy for example. But a Northeast wind of seven miles per hour is not going to factor in as much as a seventeen mile per hour blow.

So, getting back to our hypothetical Thursday,

the tide and time of day combination looks good, right? Now check to see what kind of wind is forecasted for Thursday around dusk.

Billy Batterton and his bucktail.

Right now on this trip, the right time of the tide keeps getting later and later. The last Chappy ferry stops at midnight so unless you are staying on Chappy, you will be stuck out here until 6:30 a.m.

If my son Ben was here, we would be considering it.

I notice I have been turning off the light next to my bed around 1:00 a.m. every night. Last year, with Ben, it was 3:00 a.m. every night.

Since the late Chappy tide makes it hard to catch the last ferry, I will check out what the Tide and Time looks like in Lobsterville the next few nights.

Complicated, right? Complicated and humbling. Sorry if this just got too detailed.

At least now you know why surf fishermen delight when, for a couple of days or nights, they are able to "lock in" to the right combination of Tide and Time of Day with Mother Nature letting you in and The Fish inviting you to stay.

The other way to do it is to figure out when you have time to go fishing and just go. We do that a lot as well. The place is beautiful. The Cast is magical. And the Shore Birds and Islanders are fun to be around.

RE-TIE

My favorite lure snapped off three casts ago.

And there goes the only other one I had just like it.

There are the things you do to maintain an activity, or a work project, or a friendship, or a job, or a career, or the place you live in, a vacation, or a simple avocation like this here fishing.

But sometimes the constant maintenance combined with fatigue, disappointment, and/or lack of success causes you to pause and reevaluate your commitment to it.

You find yourself having to make a decision: recommit or not.

In fishing terms, it's like the decision to Re-tie or not.

For the last few nights, I have been plagued by a constant development of wind knots. At least one or two trip-stopping knots have developed the last few nights. A wind knot can sometimes be delicately untangled or it can be more like a bird's nest requiring you to cut off all the line above the knot, wasting valuable line and reducing the amount you still need to cast well. And it slows or shuts down your fishing.

On my third night at Lobsterville, in Week Two, I had three wind knots within an hour that caused me to spend more time stripping line off my reel than actually fishing with it.

A knot snapped off my trusty green Boone needle fish thirty minutes ago. Now, this new wind knot just broke off the last spare one I had.

Maybe it is the cumulative effect of driving here, unpacking, activating, and fishing continuously that has taken its toll on me. But I cannot remember ever being so tired and disgusted.

Not even at the halfway mark of my proposed 30 night adventure and already I was being incapacitated.

I think that the expensive reel the kids gave me for Christmas is flawed.

At Lobsterville, you have to park your vehicle and walk the beach to your favorite spot. Some spots, like my favorite ones, are a long walk away. After this latest knot, I trekked back to the car disheartened, frustrated, lacking confidence and hope, and ready to quit.

Like the times you are already running on empty, already barely keeping it together, and you have to deal with the wind knot of setbacks at work, in a friendship, or with whatever it is you are invested in.

You recommit or you don't.

You re-tie or you stop.

Got in the car, saw the night was still young (9:45), took several deep breaths, poured a hot cup of coffee from the thermos, feasted on a three day old Danish, took a fifteen minute break, and regained perspective.

Decided to re-tie.

Got back out in the dark, re-tied a new leader and lure, made the long trek back to the water, and fished again for two more hours. Caught two more bass not big enough to keep, yet took much delight in being back at it.

Best of all, The Cast brought my mind back a few years when five or six fishermen came from Italy, and rented a house out here in Lobsterville. They did it for a couple of years. They fished really hard. They were in the water every time I arrived and they stayed every night after I left.

And they brought their own chef.

I was so excited to fish and interact with them because my dad came over from Italy himself.

Called my mother and asked her how to say "Good Luck" in Italian.

"In bocca al lupo," she told me.

For the next couple of nights, I would do my pretend best to sound native and what not by dropping an *"In bocca al lupo"* on one or two of them as I walked by.

Some would smile and respond. Others would grin. Some looked a bit puzzled.

But I was with my peeps now, don't you know.

Me and my ancestral peeps.

Given all kinds of *"In bocca al lupo"* to my people. Dropped *"In bocca al lupo"* like I meant it for two years in a row up here at Lobsterville when the Italians showed up.

Eventually went online and found out that *"In

bocca al lupo" translates into "into the wolf's mouth." Used a lot among Italian opera performers sort of like "break a leg."

I was telling all of them to break a leg. Thanks Ma.

And so it was that the Cast that started my night with knots around 7:00 p.m. had now moved past midnight.

Started yesterday, finished today. Halfway into my trip, it brought wonderful memories.

More importantly, I re-tied.

Attending to wind knots in work and life can cause us to lose heart. Or perspective. They present us with a moment to reevaluate and the choice to recommit or not.

You re-tie or you resign.

It's a tough spot to be in and one decision is not always better than the other.

But there is something restorative in taking a short time out to refresh.

And re-tie.

Polly Alden and her husband Dick Millett in 2008.

Polly and a striper in 2018.

CAN'T EAT AS MUCH

When you cast into the night by yourself you think of everything. Or nothing at all.

Standing alone in the dark night ocean the last few nights, I've been thinking about Bagna Caulda and Pizza.

Bagna Caulda is an ancestral family dish brought to us from Northern Italy by my grandfather Corsino Carotta. It is basically a hot anchovy dip that was served on the table in the pan fresh off the hot stove. We dipped celery and greens in it for a few minutes till it got cold. Then it was brought back to the stove and refreshed with more garlic, butter, and anchovies. Usually, we went through seven or eight pans of it before our lips looked like Lot's wife (a biblical thing there).

I have maintained the annual tradition of Bagna Caulda since childhood. Every New Year's Eve.

But now I only have the capacity to dip and slurp my way through three, maybe four refreshed pans max.

And I use to be able to scarf down a lot more slices of pizza than I can now.

We can't eat as much the older we get.

These last few nights in the water have me thinking I can't eat as much fishing as I used to. And I am struggling to admit it. Actually, I am admitting it but struggling with the decision to eat less of it. I love it so. It tastes so good and it is so gratifying. Deeply gratifying.

But too much of it makes you uncomfortable, like too much Thanksgiving food.

Consume too much fishing and it makes you just want to sleep.

Maybe one of the takeaways to this Thirty Straight is going to be that this much fishing is not for me anymore.

Glad I am doing it—will never have another opportunity to do so—but I am learning that I am not missing much by fishing less. The gorgeous stars in the sky, the moonlight on the water, and the sounds and sights of nighttime sea and surf are still there for me to consume.

But it is not good to overeat from this dish.

Maybe this is true with all our passions and hobbies and commitments and pursuits.

Best to do it when fresh and alert instead of numb and sleep walking.

Perhaps I will forget these feelings and learnings over the winter. Perhaps I will return to overdo it again next year. But at least I have marked it down here live.

In real time.

There are a few iconic Island fishermen still active after fifty years like Steve and Ed Amaral, Steve Morris, Janet Messineo, Jack Livingston, Paul Schultz, and others. But the two I have the oldest and most cherished memories of fishing with are Bernie Arruda and Cooper Gilkes.

These two were among the group back in the '70s that used to fish from the surf to help pay the rent. Standing in the surf at night after your day job with a rod and reel to help pay bills was neither romantic nor recreational. It was serious, somber, and if you were lucky enough to be around it, *formative*.

Cooper Gilkes. I first fished next to him up in Gay Head fifty years ago.

You learned how to cast in the proper direction when fishing side by side with others. You learned to pull up out of the water when the guy next to you hooked up and wait until he landed his fish before you resumed casting, no matter how badly you wanted to catch the fish in front of you. You learned to learn by watching and listening. We abstained from alcohol altogether because it required that you be fully alert and aware of multiple goings on. It is a practice I still follow. And since I am fishing night and day, that means no alcohol for me at all.

Catherine Cronin Carotta has been coming ever since we got married forty-seven years ago.

Now Catherine prefers to read and rest.
Waits all year to "hear the ocean."

Coop is known for his fishing prowess. He not only runs Coops Bait and Tackle; he was born on the Island and has a life's worth of fishing knowledge. Though we met fifty years ago up in Aquinnah, to this legend and busy fellow I am just a familiar and friendly face.

At the end of my last day last year, I asked a young man to take picture of Coop and me. It is one of my favorite fishing photos because after the photo, Coop and I stood there another thirty minutes recalling old-time events and fishermen. We were the last to leave the beach that evening.

That brief trip down years of memories was

one of the best evenings I have ever had on the water's edge.

Coop and Lela asked me how my fishing was going so far and we laughed as I told them how Billy B. and Steph Pond stopped fishing to give me multiple tutorials on jigging a bucktail.

"Must have felt sorry for me," I assured them.

I told them how Christin found the log entry that indicated those two tried to get me to try jigging twelve years ago to the day, how all I reeled in so far were weeds, and, oh yeah, lost one of Billy's personal bucktail's tails by getting hooked to a submerged boulder.

Lela giggled, Coop smiled and shook his head.

Didn't notice him getting out from behind the steering wheel and head to the back of his truck. Lela and I were still swapping stories.

Then Coop came around the truck, extended his open hand to me and said firmly, "Take this."

It was a black bucktail he had just made in his shop.

"No. No. No way. I am just going to lose it on another rock. No way. Can't waste it Coop.'

"So what. If you lose it on a rock so what. TAKE IT."

"But I don't even know how to fish with a bucktail! It's a waste Coop."

"Take it. And DON'T QUIT on jigging. DON'T QUIT."

Cooper Gilkes gives you a lure.

Not just any lure but one he *actually made himself*.

What do you do when Cooper Gilkes gives you a lure he made himself?

Dude.

WEEK THREE: JUNE 1-7

Yes, Yes, and More Yes.

"Dear Lord! These fish are kicking my butt! I can't keep up. Just kicking my butt!"

Week Three began with some of the best striped bass fishing experiences I can recall. On Chappy the night of June 1 as dusk moved into dark from 8:30-10 p.m., in front of the steps leading down from the fishermen's parking lot, (the same cliff Dad and I slid down back in 1971) I caught a striper on almost every cast for an hour and a half.

In fact, I think I may have only NOT caught a striper on three casts.

The night started with Billy Batterton looking

at my lure when I arrived and telling me, "You have the right lure on. Do not change a thing."

His protégé Aaron Hurley was to my left and he was the first to start things off. I actually heard him giggle out loud *to himself* after bringing in one HUGE fish. What a kick it is to hear a grown man giggle out loud with that kind of joy when he thinks he is alone. I am sure Aaron thought he was far enough away from everyone that no one would hear him. I will always remember the way he giggled. Pure joy.

The water was exceptionally calm and clear. Mother Nature had opened the door for us.

"Aaron, I am gonna figure this bucktail thing out tonight because it is so calm, I can feel everything."

"Correct. It's a different bite tonight. You don't have to jig the bucktail for some reason. All you have to do is reel it in slowly."

Several nights ago, Billy's father-in-law, Bill Moe, was telling anyone in earshot the same thing.

"Hey guys, I am not jigging it! Just reeling it in and I am getting fish!" So, there I was in calm, clear ocean surf finally able to maintain contact with the lure on the other end of my line. And

Aaron the pro next to me was telling me I didn't have to master the art and cadence of jigging this bucktail up and down while still maintaining the proper speed of the retrieve.

They started biting around 8:30. Each one was FAT and an inch short of a keeper. I was talking out loud to saints and angels after the fifth one, laughing all the way.

I quit counting after the twelfth. I had to remind myself to breathe as each one "walked me down the beach" twenty-five yards because of their size, strength, and my light nine foot rod.

Fighting striper after striper, walking them down, unhooking them carefully, releasing them gently, twirling around like a whirling dervish while simultaneously picking off the weed from my line as I return to my spot is a crazy, joyful, wonderful, grace filled, choreographed *dance*.

I am catching so many stripers tonight that I have to remind myself to breathe before casting again.

Aaron, well aware that I was Billy and Steph's project, was delighted.

I think I must have caught sixteen stripers before landing a beautiful thirty-two-inch keeper and going home.

Caught every single fish on the black bucktail Coop gave me from his tackle box.

Went to Coop's tackle shop the next day and asked to buy two more.

"Not for sale yet. But man are you smiling."

Then he reached underneath the counter and *gave me* two more, insisting I take them at no charge. "Given all the years you have been buying Kastmasters from me, just take 'em. The smile on your face is good enough."

That night I went back to the same spot and repeated the drill, catching eight stripers in two hours, with a keeper coming in at thirty inches.

A late-night Lobsterville bass.

A younger Ben with a Lobsterville bass in 2008.

PIVOTING

"They just shut down most of Chappy." The Martha's Vineyard Trustees of Reservations, in their annual effort to protect the piping plover, have now shut down the entire North end of Chappy. I can no longer fish the quiet Narrows, the Cedars in Pogue Pond. The Trustees are mandated by federal law to protect the hatching of piper plover, yet it seems like closing the whole entire North end of the Island is bit of an overkill. Seems like they could have found a creative way to protect birds and still maintain some limited access to the rest of the area.

I am now on the working part of my vacation, on the computer 7:00 a.m. to 2:00 p.m., fishing late afternoon for bluefish, taking a break around 7:30, switching over to my striper rod and fishing until midnight for bass.

The blues have not returned ever since their brief two-day visit weeks ago.

Christin left June 3 as planned. She is so helpful, cheerful. Intelligent, good.

The Shore Birds and the Locals all love her.

That day, while looking for bluefish, I ran into Lance and Lois Dimock. "One question," asked Lance, "Does Christin ever NOT smile? She is such a happy person."

"And we have seen her grow up over the years. Smiling every day!" added Lois.

"She loves being out here and she loves seeing everyone every year. She never cares if she catches fish, but she never stops fishing. And she ALWAYS catches the first bass among us, and always during the daytime," I said.

I was deflating my tires on Chappy earlier that day when Dick Pytko pulled over to do the same.

Dick knew I had been re-assessing whether or not I would continue the tradition next Spring given the skyrocketing rental rates and the challenge of finding a decent rental place I could afford.

Apparently, it didn't matter that I hadn't mentioned it to him in about a week.

"Can I tell you something?"

"No."

"The best reason to come back again next year is to keep spending time with your daughter. If I could fish with my daughter, I would be out here on this beach every day. I would do anything to fish with my daughter. You can't give that up. Think about that. Don't give that up."

Word this afternoon is that Washington Jim has arrived on the Island and is looking for me. To my delight, our cars cross on the beach and I fill him in on the great striper fishing of the previous two nights.

At dusk, I returned for the third night in a row to fish Wasque under the steps at the fishermen's parking lot.

Jim and his friend Larry are there. Waiting for me.

"The only reason we are here is because of what you said. And we don't want to head out there until we see where you have been fishing."

I feel the pressure. They are here based on my recommendation.

It's Billy Batterton's last night. When I get to my spot, Billy walks by and takes time to give me a more detailed tutorial on fishing the bucktail. Just before dusk turns to dark, Islander Ralph Peckham walks by and tells me how thick the bass were in the Rip up the beach "around the corner before the weeds settled in. Every cast." Ralph has taken the time to share information with me for several years now. A gesture that means so much.

I fish for an hour and a half without a hit. But that changed as soon as it got dark.

My first fish was a keeper. You can only keep one striper per day. I see this as my chance to maybe get in bed before 1:00 a.m. I pull my line up.

Billy is amazed that I am calling it a night. "One and done?"

Everyone else prefers to stay as long as the fish do, catching and releasing all but one.

"Totally. Making it an early night," I said.

But after I filet the fish, I feel responsible for Washington Jim and Larry, so I return to check on them. It's pitch black so I am walking along the shoreline trying to discern who looks like Washington Jim. First person I see is Billy, re-tying.

"On every cast since you left. Right here."

"Where's Jim?"

"Down a ways."

I find Jim.

Just then he hooks a fish. While reeling it in he adds: "Fifteen to seventeen fish, five keepers. What a first night!"

"How 'bout Larry?"

"Same thing. Thanks. Great recommendation tonight."

Crossing the Chappy Ferry around 11 p.m., I notice I have a text message on my phone. It's Ron Dumorat, a very, very good Island fisherman who has become a good fishing friend. I remember when Ron first arrived on the Island in the '80s. Green as could be, but inquisitive. I think he now holds more Daily Awards in the Martha's Vineyard Striped Bass and Bluefish Derby than anyone. Author of *Three Decades of the Derby*.

RON:

Had a good morning at the Opening, Mike. Seven fish. Four over 30 inches.

Hope to go back tomorrow morning around 4 am and you are welcome to join me.

Have you back in the car at 7am.

Ron Domurat with a 35 pounder.

THE OPENING

2:45 a.m. comes quick after less than three hours sleep. I am driving with my elbows to meet Ron for our trip to The Opening while finishing the half-eaten muffin on the front seat that I started on a day or two ago. It goes well with the lukewarm coffee still in the thermos from yesterday.

But all I can think about driving in the dark is Ralph Greenberg, my dad, and the last time I fished the Edgartown Opening back around 1979. Caught a thirty-three and a half pound striper there in the actual Opening itself (you usually fish the pools in front of the Opening). It was and is the biggest bass I ever caught. I know how much it weighed because we sold it to Ralph Greenberg who ran the busiest restaurant in Edgartown back then.

We brought it to Ralph in his kitchen where he weighed it. Paid me three dollars a pound which for us meant a hundred dollars of groceries during our trip. We needed it back then.

It turned out to be the last striper I caught for about ten years because we quit striper fishing after that. The species was in peril, a moratorium was put on catching stripers, followed by a new minimum of thirty-six inches. As visitors with only two weeks of vacay, we lacked the knowledge to find big bass and did not want to waste nights guessing where to go. So, we just focused on blues for those years.

I am sure it is also why I fish so hard for stripers today.

But I am also thinking of Ralph because it was the first time I had ever been inside a commercial kitchen. Having grown up in a food centric but small apartment, I was wide eyed. I clearly remember that moment when Ralph showed us how to filet a fish properly, and insisted we do so "with just one cut."

A technique I have never mastered.

I am flooded with wonderful memories of the Opening as Ron and I fish it. Dawn breaks and it is beautiful. Ron gets a fish but I do not. No matter. It is breathtaking and refreshing to be here at sunrise with a good friend, veteran fisherman, and the sea.

Ron has me back at 7:00 a.m. as promised. It is Sunday, so I head to Church then the Black Dog to grab the Sunday Boston Globe and New York Times.

I go to bed at 10:00 in the morning with a plan: bookend this morning's sunrise fishing with a sunset fishing trip to Lobsterville. I already know that the tide will not be great at that time but sunset sometimes trumps the tide there in Lobsterville. Seems fitting to follow a sunrise trip with a sunset one on the same day. Plus, I get to wake up later this afternoon and read the Sunday papers.

The sunset trip at Lobsterville does not result in a fish. But as dusk turns to dark, I realize it is the first night where I can see my shadow on the sand, thanks to the sliver of a growing moon.

Pull my line out around 10:00 p.m. and make it home in time to see the last few minutes of the Celtics-Warriors game.

What a wonderful Sunday this was. Sunrise and sunset on the water. Church and rest, the Sunday papers reconnecting me to the world, and the Celtics in the finals.

No wonder everyone is encouraging all of us to develop more Mindfulness, Gratitude, and learn how to Be In The Moment.

I get it.

It does add color and richness to the elements of life that can sustain us.

At the Edgartown Opening 1979.

Christin's first bass on the rod she built. 38" 11 p.m. 5/20/12 East Beach.

THE CAST

A swimmer's stroke. A jogger's pace. A marching band's cadence. A baker's kneading. The yoga poses. Mindful breathwork. A walker's stride.

Physical movements and actions that are meditative.

Contemplation in the midst of motion.

Properly developing these physical movements demands endless days of practice. Each person executes one or another in their own way.

They can be done alone or with others who have the discipline.

Once mastered, these movements work their magic on the mind, the heart, the spirit.

Like the cast of the surf fishermen throwing lures and retrieving them from the water's edge.

The physical movement of casting, for fifteen minutes or seventy-five, opens fishermen up to the pondering, the evaluating, the remembering, the admitting, the resolving, the planning that comes with contemplation.

Casting also moves the surfcaster to the place where after a year's worth of noise, one's Inner Voice can be heard and responded to.

In the Cast you get lost.

You cannot seem to control where The Cast takes you. It can take you to the past or the future. Often though it takes you to the balcony where you can gaze down on the dancing and drama of your life and the lives of those you love. From the balcony, the Cast provides a view you may not get often in daily life. You can see who you may need to include more often, or who may be stepping on toes, or whether the pace of your life's interactions and tasks needs to be slowed down, or picked up.

In the Cast, you also get found.

Whatever, wherever, or whomever is Home, you can see it from the Cast.

The Cast brings clarity as to what in your

work or family or world is worth your effort, worth your worry, worth your commitment.

And occasionally, surfcasters will let you into that space by sharing something they have been thinking about, remembering, or claiming as True. Such sharing is unsolicited most of the time. The surfcaster just lets you into the contemplative space created by the Cast.

It is plain as day among the surfcasting community on the Vineyard in the Spring. There are seldom loud parties or barbeques. It is more of a quiet culture where fishermen speak only when they are not engaged in The Cast. The voices are never loud or boisterous, except for those delightfully insane and wonderfully exhilarating bluefish or bass blitz. In the middle of a blitz, The Cast is accompanied by narrators who giggle at the burst of white water behind their lures and the onset of The Tug.

Most of the world mistakenly assumes that casting is about catching fish. All surfcasters know better, save the novice or weekender hurrying toward some sort of capture or accomplishment.

You can witness it in the silence among those engaged in the cast.

You can see it in the private space they each stake out among themselves.

For themselves.

MOM AND DAD DAYS

The next two days, June 6 and 7 are dedicated to my mom and dad.

Anne Carotta.

Anne Carotta loved the Vineyard. She cherished the way Islanders Dottie and Roy Gundersen set aside two weeks in their rental every Spring for thirty-five years and never raised the rent. When the Gundersen's sold one rental and moved to a new one they always set aside a few weeks for us. We watched the Gundersen family move through life's passages much like they watched ours. Knowing that Dottie and Roy would always set aside a few weeks for us gave Anne, and all of us, a tradition she shared with all who cared to join us. Watching Kevin and Jeff Gundersen grow from children to adults made this more than transactional: it became relational.

Mom passed four years ago around 10:00 p.m. while Ben and I were fishing Chappy near a spot called Metcalf's—where Ray Metcalf and his wife caught a fifty-four pound Derby-winning bass in 1974.

I always make sure to fish that same spot at 10:00 p.m. every June 6.

Just about dusk, I arrive at Metcalf's, check my phone before leaving the car, and see a text from Janet Messineo, whom I haven't texted since the first night's query about fishing at Tashmoo.

Janet is a wonderful person and a terrific,

determined fisherman. Her book, *Casting Into the Light* is an authentic and soulful account of her journey through life in surf here on the Island.

> JANET:
>
> Hey Mike what's been going on here today.
>
> I'm going out to the Rip now. Have you been getting into the bass I am hearing about?

> ME:
>
> Hi Janet. Just fished the falling tide 3 hrs. for bluefish. Nothing.
>
> Got into bass at Wasque for three nights but bite slowed down a bit it seems.
>
> Was good right after the turn but it got too late for the Chappy ferry.
>
> I will now try turning into the rising.

Out at Metcalf's I had trouble standing in the surf. With the beach sloped so high behind me, it was like a washing machine. You're hit in the front with waves coming in and then almost pulled off your heels from behind as the waves come down the slope behind you and rush back down to the sea, pulling the sand away from under your feet it rushes past.

There were no fish at Metcalf's for me on June 6.

Mom and I had a great visit.

Under the stars and the light of the growing moon, I told her once again how much I loved her and that she was the kindest, best woman I had ever known in my whole life.

She smiled several times.

I reached for the phone to let my wife Catherine know I was heading home. There was another message from Janet:

> JANET:
>
> Nothing for me tonight.
>
> My friend Steve got one little schoolie and then it got really weedy.
>
> But what a beautiful evening. I'm going home now.
>
> Were you out?

ME:

> Just returning on the Chappy ferry now. Nada.

JANET:

> I just left before you then. A beautiful fishless night.

For an Islander and professional like Janet, the beauty of the sea and sky at night is as captivating as the creatures we seek to catch.

I too loved the night sky tonight. There were plenty of stars in the sky and the moon kept increasing in size.

So if you are ever able to fish Martha's Vineyard on a clear night, here's is the only advice you will find in this book:

Look up.

TRIBUTE

It is 2017. I am fishing near a spot where an elderly Ray Metcalf and his wife caught a winning striper of fifty-four pounds. Mr. Metcalf, as I called him, actually caught that fish in a different spot than the one so many fishermen have now named Metcalf's Hole. He once caught a forty-three pound bass that , in it's mouth, still had the lure it snapped off of Kib Bramhall's line a day or so earlier on another part of the Island. I still see eighty-year-old Mr. Metcalf and his tiny white haired wife in their blue truck in my mind's eye every time someone mentions Metcalf's Hole.

Anyway, here at Metcalf's there is a fisherman to my right.

I had no idea who this guy was, but for three straight evenings, he showed up and fished next to me. On the first night he explained he was trying out a new rod and reel the tackle shop wanted to sell him. The next night he showed me the reel he ended up buying.

"An upgrade from the one I tried out yesterday."

He couldn't catch a thing but he was determined. Stood in the waves four and five hours each evening. He was worried he wasn't casting far enough, not reeling at the right speed, just not doing something right. Had a good natured way of making fun of himself for his lack of luck. After the second night he went to a different tackle shop for more advice and reassurance. By the third evening he was attached to my hip.

Over the waves and the wind and the rain and the gorgeous sunsets he told of his long, brutal winter. After twenty-five years, and without warning, his wife had left him.

He is off to a new start this Spring. He and a friend now have a five hundred dollar diet bet on who would lose the most weight.

"My mother found out and told me that if I win the bet she'd throw in another five hundred.

I said Mom. Really? Really mom? Am I that overweight? But I have been trying to lose weight for years now…. And I put all the booze in the basement."

There was a weighty tone to that last statement.

"Developed some bad habits. Unhealthy habits. Stupid habits. But in the winter when it gets dark by 4:30 …" His voice trailed off, he took a breath, shook his head, and sighed. "It's rough."

Once again, we made cast after cast, assured each other, and waited for the fish.

Then his rod bent.

I cheered.

As the fish ran hard and tested his newly purchased gear, he held his rod high, leaned back against it, looked over at me and smiled contently. Serenely. Peacefully.

I pulled my line out of the water just to watch him.

This wasn't about catching a fish. This was about overcoming.

He didn't rush. He soaked it in. Took his time. Other guys waited for him to hurry up and land the thing so they could resume fishing.

He didn't seem to see them. Maybe he didn't care.

He just smiled and took his time, totally focused on the fish at the end of his line.

"Nice fish! BEAUTY." I said as it finally made it to the beach.

Three nights of casting, multiple consults, purchases, second-guessing, and perseverance had paid off.

"Winter's over Duke! Winter's over! Congratulations!"

"It *IS* a beauty." He said as he admired the bluefish on the beach. *"Beautiful fish.* Wish I could eat it."

Before I could say, "It would be great for your diet," he gently held it in his hands and reverently brought it back to the water.

Then in a voice louder than the one he used for three nights.

Loud like making an announcement.

Like making a proclamation.

Loud like that.

Formal loud.

"I release this fish in memory of Patrick Gregory. He was a good man and my good friend."

He was announcing it loud enough for the God of the Sea and the Fish and the Souls and the Universe to hear it.

Loud enough for those who wished they were present to hear it.

He was announcing it aloud so that all the angels and saints could hear it.

Loud enough so he himself could hear it.

Sometimes a moment takes your breath away, your draw drops, your eyes widen, you pause.

But this was the other kind of moment.

The kind of moment you inhale and take it in because it is for your soul.

And the older your soul the better it gets at letting you know when to automatically take it in.

I actually felt myself breathe it in.

The intimate gesture of Paying Tribute.

The way we honor someone of virtue. The way we recognize… celebrate…call out someone who has graced our lives. Cooperstown and Springfield are not the only places that have a Hall of Fame.

Our hearts have a Hall of Fame, too.

He watched the fish swim away and explained, "I made a promise that I would release the first fish I caught this year for my good friend. He wasn't a fisherman. He was a golfer." He laughed. "But he was my good friend and a great man."

As witness to the three nights of hard work, the effort, expense, and doggedness, I swallowed and said slowly, clearly, carefully, purposely.

"Then you are a man of your word, Duke."

"I am that," he said. And added nothing more.

I turned away to face the sea and the sky and welled up.

You know grace when you see it.

FAREWELL AND THANK YOU

"You are in a good spot here."

One a.m. on a dark night in the late '70s. Forty-five years ago.

A solitary shadow approaches Dad and me from our left, walking from a parking lot that is nearly a mile away. I am in my twenties. It is Bernie Arruda. He is my hero and his word is gold.

This spot is in the middle of a long stretch of beach that is not marked. You don't just park here and fish. To get to this spot you must drive past it, park in a small lot a half a mile down the highway, walk back along the highway to a small trail that went over the dunes to the beach. The hallowed spot on the beach was actually in a bend or "bowl" with deep water directly in front of you.

Dad and I found it accidentally. That night Bernie affirmed our discovery.

Tonight, I decide to return to that special strip of beach in Lobsterville to celebrate my dad, who passed away on this day years ago.

He and I would talk about this spot all year long until we were able to return here.

I have three moments enshrined in my memory box from this one spot.

We were fishing there one night forty years ago when a man walked over the dune and appeared next to us just as the sun was getting ready to go down. He explained that he was a Native Wampanoag elder from Aquinnah. I have come to think he was an elder from the Vanderhoop family.

He had no waders, no raincoat, no tackle box.

Just his rod, reel, and lure.

He quietly made two casts and landed a large weakfish, probably seven or eight pounds.

"Dinner," he said, and was gone.

Man knew exactly what he was doing. He knew when and where and how to catch dinner and spent all of ten minutes doing it. We had been there several nights. Several hours every night. No weakfish for us. Dad and I reminded ourselves of this for years.

Then Bernie Arruda, who grew up on the Island as well, showed up in the middle of that night back over forty years ago. He had walked at least a mile in the middle of the night and would have to walk back afterwards. Alone. Always alone. And smoking an occasional cigar.

We had met Bernie in Gay Head on our second trip in 1972. He began to befriend us.

Bernie Arruda was my favorite fisherman. He would quietly answer my fishing questions with only half a sentence. It was never enough. But I was too intimidated to ask for clarification. I persisted with more questions and he did not seem to mind, even if he never fully elaborated on any of his answers.

Dad and I knew nothing in those early years. But Bernie knew everything. Our strategy was always to "Find Bernie" as early in the annual trip as possible, ask him where and how to fish, and set our plans from there.

The three of us fished this hallowed spot every spring for several years. Dad and I would talk all winter about finding the unmarked path over the dune, emerging through the brush to our enchanted beach, fishing with Bernie, and reminding ourselves of what Bernie taught us about the light lures: "Reel it as slowly as you can. Set the hook on the bump."

About ten years ago, I saw Bernie fishing off the Edgartown Big Bridge so I pulled over. He had gotten old and explained that his knees couldn't stand the pounding of the surf any longer. Plus, the cost of a beach sticker and maintenance on a 4-wheel drive was getting too much.

Besides, he explained, he was able to catch bass here off the bridge anyway.

> So, I was fishing here last Spring and I could see the bass feeding but they wouldn't take anything. For an hour. Bass everywhere but not taking anything I would throw 'em.
>
> Then I saw birds diving. They were feeding on a nice school of bunker.
>
> So, I took off my lure and switched to a weighted treble hook. You know what I am talking about?

I fished under the birds and snagged a bunker with the weighted treble.

Broke its back, kept it on the treble and threw it back in the water. Bass were all over it. Caught three bass on the same bunker, including a thirty-five-pounder.

While working on my doctorate in Leadership Education I studied how leadership involves good responses to Adaptive Challenges.

For years I shook my head recalling how Bernie Arruda responded so organically to an Adaptive Challenge. But I am also amazed by the way he calmly explained it to me as if it was the logical thing to do.

As if everyone knows to:

- notice the birds
- identify what they are feeding on
- stop fishing
- change to a weighted treble
- snag the bait fish (you have to drag the weighted treble through the school of bait to snag one)
- break its back so it can't swim away from a predator

- use it to catch the predator

Yeah, okay.

The third moment enshrined in my memory box was the striper Dad caught in this very spot on Lobsterville beach in the early '80s. In the car on the way to this spot that night, we had just discussed the importance of setting your drag just right—before fishing—and refraining from tightening the drag while fighting a hooked fish. Then, thirty minutes later, he was hooked up with a drag, pulling big one.

I pulled out just to watch him. And sure enough he had enough discipline to NOT tighten the drag. Instead, he patiently stayed with it, letting the big fish do its thing, pulling drag once and again for fifteen minutes until it finally was his. It weighed thirty-seven and a half pounds *the next morning*. Given the water loss and dehydration overnight, my guess it was a forty pounder.

Within a few minutes I, too, was hooked up with what we both thought was another huge bass. Instead it was the biggest bluefish we had ever seen. We had always estimated it was close to twenty pounds. Those two fish are the largest my family has ever caught. Largest bass and largest blue we have ever landed and both came from this place on that same night.

I have only been back to this spot once since Dad died twenty-one years ago. Here again now, I am thinking of Dad and Bernie and the truly golden years we fished here. It is *not the same* without them. I walked it left and right as I fished it from 6:00 p.m. till sunset. But the sunset could not outweigh the fact it was dead low tide. No fish tonight. I pulled my line out before it got dark so I could settle in at the Menemsha Channel nearby and fish it when it got dark.

Walking off, I deliberately turned to say goodbye to this hallowed place.

But I had to turn around two more times because of what I saw.

It looked different. It no longer had the look or *the feel* of the weathered natural beach I remembered.

I turned around again until I could figure out what made it look different.

You know how empty your house looks after you have cleaned everything out of it and gotten it ready for the people you sold it to?

You may have lived there for twenty-five years but once it is empty it looks differently than the way you have become accustomed to seeing it, like you have never seen it this way before.

And it looks ready for the next inhabitants.

That's exactly what I saw in this spot as I turned around to say goodbye. I had to turn around several times in order to figure out why and how it looked different.

Those of us who lived here before are already gone.

The place is now ready for the next inhabitants.

Farewell and Thank You. Dear place. Dear people. Dear times.

Dad's 37.5 lb Lobsterville bass circa 1980.

Spontaneous reunion with Bernie Arruda at the Edgartown dock in 2003. It had been years since we had last seen each other.

WEEK FOUR: JUNE 8-15
MEDITATION

"Looks like mustard and ketchup."

I arrive at Chappy to fish for afternoon blues at the start of week four and find Coop out there giggling about a new yellow and red bucktail he has created.

"It's got wings on it! Look." He says as he reveals something coming out the side of the bucktail.

"Looks like ketchup and mustard," I said. "Think it will work?"

"Dunno," he giggles. "Gonna give it a try."

I'm worried about Coop. He seems to be having fun out here.

My wife Catherine was able to work from here for two weeks but now she has returned home.

That means I will spend the rest of the time fishing ten hours a day, usually in three and a half hour segments. It's a system I look forward to.

Work at my computer from 7:30 to 1:30. Then fill the small cooler with sandwiches, chicken salad, muffins, water, and an ice pack. Fill the thermos and the mug with coffee, drop some ice packs in the big cooler in case I catch blues, and off I go.

Then two segments bluefishing: 2:30-5:00 then 5:30-7:30.

Night segment 8:00 p.m. to midnight fishing for bass. In bed around 1:00 a.m.

As week four begins, the blues still do not show. I have never seen them arrive so late. Used to be that I would take bluefish to The Net Result in May but never in June. The last couple of years it's reversed. No May bluefish, only June bluefish. On this trip Christin and I caught bluefish twice in May. Nothing since then and it's now June 8.

As I switch over to my light bass rod and bucktail, Steph Pond, still trying to help his slow learning student, tells me I have the wrong color tail on my black bucktail.

"You need black. A black tail. All black."

He reaches into a jar for a black tail.

"No. No. No. I'm all set."

"Here for Pete's sake. It's a nickel a tail. Take off the white one and put this on."

"Okay. THANK YOU."

"You're WELCOME."

We fish in front of the steps at Wasque as dusk turns into night. Nothing but weeds again.

It dawns on me that it has been four days and nights since I caught a fish. That's a lot of hours in the water without any luck. I am wearing out physically and mentally.

Steph tells me he is going to fish the Pogue Gut since the tide has turned there and it should be running well now.

I stay where I am for another hour then head to the Gut to see what's going on.

"No fish here," Steph says as I make my way down the steps at the Gut.

We fish together thirty minutes until Steph leaves.

"Take care, Nebraska."

"You too, Steph. Thanks for everything."

"Thank you," he says.

I did not see Steph again the rest of my trip.

He made a real intentional effort to bring me into the work of jigging bucktails and I hope he knows how grateful I am. We all remember when he first arrived on the Island and everyone agrees how much he has developed into an elite fisherman—with both a bucktail and his fly rod.

I fished 8-11:15 p.m. on June 9 and caught two schoolie bass. This is a term used to describe juvenile bass. Bass that are almost keeper size are often referred to as Shorts. I decided to try and keep track of the bass I caught on this thirty-day thing of mine but I quit counting around forty-two bass last week on Lobsterville. By now I am in the fifties.

These are the only schoolies I've caught so far.

All the other fish have been Shorts, which is a good sign that perhaps the local striper population is coming back a little from the edge of endangerment.

The sea—and fishing its surf—has a mediative power.

And it always brings clarity.

I am reminded of this while taking a break outside the car out at Wasque next to another fisherman. He and I have been the only ones fishing there the previous two hours.

I do not know him. He introduces himself as Joe, and after we exchange short summaries of our fishing experience that day, he moves right into a story about his dad.

He explains that his dad was quite a storyteller and would refer to his college athletic achievements from time to time. Joe tells me of his dad's military service and the crazy way he just enrolled in one college and then the next, eventually spending the last few years at Bucknell before graduating there.

Joe goes on to explain that he reached out to Bucknell on a whim a few years ago, just to see if they had any details about his late dad's involvement in athletics.

Bucknell informed Joe that his dad was the starting quarterback on the school's last unbeaten team, and given that most players played both offense and defense in those days, his dad was also the star linebacker for the team that only gave up ten points the entire season.

This story from this stranger has no connection at all to the fishing we had been doing.

What it does reveal is that the fishing had brought Joe back to these memories and he could not help but verbalize them to someone in that moment.

The sea, and fishing its surf, has meditative power. As I have said before it brings Liminal space. I had walked into someone's meditative, Liminal space, and he couldn't help but speak from that space. I was honored to witness it.

Phil Bibeau of New Hampshire with a bluefish. Spends the day quietly sitting next to his truck with his dog. Doesn't matter if fish arrive.

THE ENVELOPE

For a couple of weeks every trip—usually the last two weeks of May—I inhabit the role of a commercial fisherman, taking my catch to the local fish market called The Net Result.

All the "fish money" and all the receipts stay in an old worn out little envelope. We use the money to replenish fishing equipment, hot coffee, and an occasional tank of gas.

We've been doing it since college and it somehow keeps me connected to those ole fishermen who taught me how to do it.

At the end of the vacation, the envelope goes into the tackle box and is not opened again until we return the next year. Some years I forget to cash the check.

Our one rule is that the "fish money" only be spent in the community from which it came.

But that worn-out envelope holds way more than money. The money itself is like monopoly money, helping us to keep playing a game we love.

What that envelope really holds is The Narrative.

Years of memories scribbled on receipts, like "520 lbs. to market in 2006", "759 lbs. in 2014" as well as handwritten notes and directions to new spots someone told us about.

It holds the joyful contribution visiting nieces and nephews made by catching their first fish. "Michael and Anthony fished here for the first time." "Analise caught her first bluefish."

It's not an envelope with money.

It is a memory box.

And every time I hold it, those memories fill me with gratitude.

At the car wash one day in 2009, while vacuuming out the sand and snatching up plastic lunch bags, crumpled coffee cups, old fishing line and God knows what, I accidentally threw out the envelope when I emptied my pockets.

Didn't realize it until I got back home.

Raced back in a panic to the car wash only to see the garbage truck driving off with the garbage.

Followed the truck to its next stop, where the driver handed me a broom handle and allowed me to dig into the bowels of the truck's wet garbage to find it.

Recognized all the trash from my car but not the envelope. I dug some more.

No luck.

The weight of my sadness surprised me.

The family couldn't figure out why I was so sad.

"It's only money. Not like someone got hurt or your truck broke down. You're still on vacation. You can still go fishing every day."

But it was not so.

"Ever lose a memory box?"

"So," they said. "Start again."

Later that day, I drove up and down the beach to my favorite spots, watched the tides and tried to start again. Brought my fresh fish to The Net Result again the next morning like a preoccupied zombie. Walked through the back door, called out to Lou Larsen to announce my arrival but stopped mid-sentence.

On the wall next to the phone was a yellow Post It with my name on it and a message: Call the police station.

"We have something that belongs to you," said the dispatcher.

Rushed to the station and straight to the front desk.

There was the envelope.

"I won't take this money if you can't tell me who turned it in."

"No problem." The cop smiled. "He left his card."

The envelope was exactly as I had left it. Full of wrinkled old receipts, handwritten notes, dates, and summaries in three different colors of ink, and the money.

It was found by the Reverend David Christensen from the United Church of Christ in Edgartown. His card said that he specialized in Ministries in Ghana, West Africa.

I called this stranger immediately.

"Where was it?"

"In the top of the trash can. I noticed it just

before I threw out my own trash. Once I saw the receipts, I realized it was some fisherman's catch. I was running a lot of last minute errands since I'm leaving for Ghana in three days, so I took it to the police station on my way home."

"But didn't you think like, 'Thank you, Lord! Found money! What a gift! Just in time to share with the poor in Africa!'"

"No. Not for a second," said the minister. "All I thought about was that someone lost their hard-earned money."

"I want to make a donation for your trip. Where can I meet you?"

"Just stop by the Church and give it to the secretary. I'll be stopping in there later tomorrow anyway."

"And I got some fish for you."

"Great! We'll grill it tomorrow night! People from the church are coming over to wish us luck before we go."

Wrote Reverend Christensen a personal check for about half the amount of the fish money in the envelope and went down to his Church to drop it off. But no one was there. Saw a box of canned goods and clothes labeled "Ghana Mission," so I taped the check to the box.

Next, I went to the kitchen and left the fish in the refrigerator, with David's name on it.

Got a call on my cell while driving along the beach the next day.

"Thanks for the check. It was generous. We'll share it with our friends in Ghana. And thanks for the fish. They were so fresh! Delicious. Incredible." He laughed.

Got out of the truck and began casting. The sun was bright, the water was a beautiful blue. The sound of the surf was friendly again. No bites. No matter. I celebrated.

Cast after rhythmic cast into the ocean, all I could think about was how two individuals each chose to exercise their integrity. And all sorts of folks got blessed.

I got my memory box back, the minister got a couple of hundred bucks and some fish, plus the people of Ghana got some extra help. 1x1=100

So now there is a new multiplication story in the envelope. Bigger than all the others.

A modern version of the Loaves and Fishes.

The children started at an early age. Aaron top, Ben bottom.

CATCHING BEAUTY

I count 24 fly fishermen to my right and left. Fishing results the next two days were exactly the same. Despite ten hours in the water each day, there were no bluefish during the day and no bass at night. It feels like I have been fishing alone on the water the last week or so.

The Shore Birds are all gone and the Islanders don't seem to be fishing the same time or places as I am.

On Saturday evening, June 11, my twenty-fifth night of fishing, I make the forty-minute drive back up to a popular strip of beach at Lobsterville and cast from 7-10:30. Looking ahead at the tide and time combinations, I think this will be the last night I fish here. The tide appears to be a bit more attractive back on Chappy the rest of the week.

Fly fishermen line the beach. More than I have ever seen in one place. They are all spaced out a proper distance from each other. All are focused on their sport. There is no conversation among them, only the sound of their fly rods whipping back and forth.

The sun sets in your face when you fish Lobsterville and Menemsha.

As it sets tonight, it is breathtakingly beautiful.

I notice the fisherman to my right has pulled out of the water and is using his phone to record the sunset.

Then I notice two other fly fishermen in his party are doing the same, while still standing waist-high in the water. They have reached into their waders to pull out their phones, and while clutching rods under their arms, without a word, each has stopped fishing to record the sunset.

This is another sign of this new generation of fishermen. They are aware of the beauty. Catching aspects of it is as valuable to them as catching fish.

I myself am just giddy to be fishing in clear, weedless water, on a beautiful Saturday night with a ton of fishermen around, allowing me to see if the fish themselves invite us to stay. Mother Nature has definitely opened her arms to us all tonight.

Don't know if the fish themselves will invite us to stay, but I'm delighted with Mother Nature's hospitality.

Twenty minutes after the sun disappeared, I noticed the fisherman on my right, the one who first recorded the sunset, caught two nice bass.

I pulled up and walked over to him, breaking the silence.

"So cool to see you catch the sunset before catching two fish."

"I was waiting on that sunset. Did not want to miss it."

He introduced himself as Chuck from Albany, New York. He and his buddies were there for the week.

The others in his party left once it got dark.

He and I continued on.

I caught two shorts around 10 p.m.

"What did you switch to?"

"An old Boone needlefish. I have been waiting till dark to throw it."

"They hit it immediately," Chuck said, revealing that he had been fishing with one eye on his lure and one on mine.

He went to his gear bag and pulled one out.

"Chuck! That green one is absolutely my favorite. I lost two last week so I am using this dark blue one, but man that green one is the best."

"Yeah, that's what Coop told me too."

"You go to Coop's?"

"Yeah, we stop there when we first get to the Island and then again after a couple of days."

"Next time you go to Coop's tell him you were fishing up at Lobsterville with Mike from Nebraska."

"Will do."

The 10 p.m. bite lasted about twenty minutes which supports a theory I have formulated on years' worth of notes in my log: night tides contain a twenty-minute active bite period where the fish feed actively and then stop for the next hour or two.

You miss that twenty-minute bite, and you may be a long time in the water without a hit.

Unless the fish invite you to stay.

Steph Pond on his flyrod when not on his bucktail.

GRATITUDE

"You know you are driving around with your raincoat hanging off the side of your car, right?"

My final Sunday starts off great. Church at 8 a.m., groceries at 9. Make a thermos plus a mug of coffee, pack the cooler with lunch and dinner, and grab the Sunday Boston Globe to read during ebb tide out on Chappy. Fish again 12-12.

On Chappy, I meet a party of three from Wilmington, Delaware. Steve, his dad Mike, and their grandson.

Steve and I fish next to each other from noon til two. We chat on and off since the blues are not around. Even though I have never met him before, he explains that he has just retired and he and his wife have moved to Rehoboth Beach. Says the year has been rough.

"Retired. Sold the house. Purchased the new one in Rehoboth. Then my mom died. We had to sell her house. Move all her things out. Take care of all her affairs, plus our own ... I lost eighteen pounds burying my mom, buying and selling, moving, ordering furniture. Came up here just to breathe, if you know what I mean."

"I do actually. Went through the same thing myself last year. Lost weight. Couldn't sleep. Too many details to manage."

"Exactly."

A few days ago it was a stranger talking about his football-playing Dad. Today another stranger talks about his stress.

The sea, the surf, the salt air, the sun, the sounds.

The Cast.

They have the power to open a person up.

Afterward, I trek down the beach "around the corner" and cast another seventy-five minutes for bluefish.

Nothing.

When I return to the Car, Steve says they have

been into bluefish ever since I left. He and his party had eighteen BIG bluefish.

The blitz was now over.

After three weeks of fishing every day for bluefish, I had missed them. Walked the wrong way. They blitzed here and I had simply fished "around the corner."

Christin texts me to see how things are going. I tell her I just missed BIG blues. And then I tell her I am almost FISHED OUT.

In our family this is a grave term usually meant to mean

DONE.

OVER.

FINISHED.

We never use this term. We usually just let each other know when we are close to it. It is our way of indicating we are in need of a serious break or we will not be able to go on.

An SOS.

As dusk approached, a fisherman wrapping up his bluefish gear calls my attention to the raincoat hanging from the top of my car.

I had hung it on my rod rack to air out six hours earlier when I arrived and forgot it was still there.

I poured a cup of coffee, grabbed a sandwich and took a break before switching over to my bass rod, night light, etc. I was staring at the ocean in my windshield when Ed Amaral stuck his head in the open window on the passenger's side.

My kids and I love eighty-six-year-old Ed Amaral. He and his brother Steve are legendary Island fishermen. They and their dad were actually the first to ever weigh in a bass at the very first Martha's Vineyard Striped Bass and Bluefish Derby in 1946. That picture is still used in Derby promotional material.

Three or four years ago, Ed won the top prize in the Derby: a new truck. His brother Steve is in the Derby Hall of Fame, too. They are among the very best, iconic, Islander fishermen.

Several years ago, Ed told me a story:

1983, in his prime, Ed caught what he felt was a world record fish on thin, four pound test line from the rocky shores under the Gay Head lighthouse.

He sent the evidence and the facts to the International Game Association. They told him his record catch did not count because of what they saw as a technicality. There was no distinction between fish landed from shore and fish caught from a boat. They pointed out that someone on a boat had a bigger fish on four pound line than the one Ed landed on the rocky shore of Gay Head.

Ed felt it was not fair to place shore and boat catches in the same category.

So Ed took the time and effort to write them a long response to their decision.

On toilet paper.

And sent it to them.

Now he sticks his big grinning face inside the Car window and asks me how I did with the blues this afternoon.

"Missed 'em, Ed. I fished around the corner the whole time and had no idea they were here."

We both laughed.

"Ain't that some shit," he said, laughing and shaking his head.

I knew he was worried about the health of his partner Lois. He told me a week or so ago that she had been hospitalized. I asked him how she was doing.

His ever-grinning countenance and tone went entirely solemn.

"She's doing as well as she can. She's in the

car with me today so that's a good sign. You know, it is what it is. You deal with the hand you get. You know?"

But then his voice changed and his face lit up again. He repeated something he seems to say every year:

"But man, I am GRATEFUL every day, man! Every day I am so grateful! You see the world as it is today and the misery experienced by so many." He shakes his head. "You have to be grateful. Things could change in a second. In a second things could change. So I am so grateful. I thank the Man Upstairs every day."

He was as animated and authentic as always. Repeating something he has told me every year since I first met him.

"You know Ed, I have been thinking about that. I keep trying to remind myself to be more grateful. You are absolutely right. And I gotta work on it," I confessed.

"It's okay, man. At least you're there (aware of it)!"

It is something I needed to hear and needed to admit. Good medicine for someone almost Fished Out.

I am ashamed of myself actually. Look at me.

Got to spend thirty days fishing on Martha's Vineyard.

With family and friends. Plus still able to "work from home a little."

And struggling to be grateful! My how we can lose sight of what we have been given.

As he departed, we urged each other to Stay Well.

Ed explained years ago that he never says Goodbye.

86-year-old Ed Amaral with a Wasque Blue at dusk.

SEEING THE UNSEEN

Ron Domurat and Dick Pytko were behind me in the Chappy Ferry line. Word had gone out about blues the day before and now the Chappy Ferry line was twenty cars long.

I never thought I would have a chance to spend a Monday afternoon shooting the breeze with these two Islanders. They are nice guys I have known for a long time. Standing outside our cars on the long Chappy line, for the first time ever, I felt like a local Islander instead of a visitor.

Dick Pytko is a Vietnam veteran. No one knows that he has been a guardian angel for other veterans on the Island. Specifically, he has helped them get the disability payments they earned in combat.

He has helped four that I know of: fishermen friends who were disabled in combat and had not followed up on the paperwork needed to collect their disability payments.

A few years ago he told me about one of the fishermen from the old group of Islanders that used to rod and reel from the surf to help pay rent. Forty years ago that particular fisherman built his beautiful house with material he gleaned from the dump. Dick spent years trying to get the guy to apply for his earned credit. When Dick finally helped him secure a lump sum reimbursement for missed disability payments, the man was afraid to cash the check, fearing that Veterans Affairs would realize they had made a mistake and come back for it. Dick not only got the guy the check, he had convinced him not to be afraid to cash it.

He helped another Islander drive to Rhode Island to get proper medical care. Got in the car with the guy and rode with him for support.

And then he convinced an Islander that he should file for the one hundred percent disability he earned in Vietnam—even if he didn't need the money—so that the VA Office would still know how much to budget every year. Reluctantly, that Vietnam veteran followed Dick's urging and as soon has he started getting a check every month, he gave it to other veterans needing assistance. This fellow has never kept one of those checks for himself. He gives every one of them to another needy veteran—typically a young one fresh from recent wars in Afghanistan.

These are stories one never hears. Good works that go unseen. Like keeper bass below the surface.

I complement Dick for the hard work he has done on behalf of so many.

"I am not a religious man in the traditional way. But I do believe in helping people when I get the opportunity to do so."

Told him that was religious enough for me.

The blues returned that afternoon like clockwork and everyone was there waiting for them. I caught seven BIG in a seventy-five minute bite and took them to The Net Result.

Turned right around and headed back to Chappy in hopes of catching a bass under the Strawberry moon I have been waiting for. I parked again at the fishermen's parking lot and walked down the stairs to my spot. There were several other fishermen there already. As the moon came up, guys started taking out their camera phones again just like the crew in Lobsterville did with the sunset a few nights ago.

Later everyone said they thought the shrimp boats on the horizon were on fire as the pink Strawberry moon began to rise behind them.

Caught and released several bluefish at dusk. Then the bass showed up and it was wonderful. Caught maybe seven or eight until landing a beautiful thirty-two inch keeper at 9:45.

A few days ago I was almost Fished Out and I thought for sure that I would not be able to catch another keeper.

Today changed all that.

Got to hang out with locals like a local all afternoon.

Caught nice bluefish and got to take them to the market.

Caught plenty of nice bass under the Strawberry moon.

Ended the day and night with this beautiful keeper.

I am so grateful.

Mother Nature had welcomed us in.

And the fish invited us to stay.

The next day the blues returned for the third straight day and I took five to the market. Ralph Peckham approached me with a nice ten-pound blue and a plea:

"It swallowed the hook and I couldn't release it. I want to give it away but I am afraid that since it is so big it may not get treated well. Will you take it?"

"Ralph, I never take fish from anyone. Never have."

"I know. I know, but we all thought you would treat it properly."

"Ralph, I would be going to the market with it."

"I know but at least it would be properly treated and enjoyed."

So I broke a long standing rule for the first time since Ed Jerome in 1981 and let someone else give me a bluefish.

This would be the fourth trip and final trip to the market in the thirty-day adventure. Christin and I had brought in twenty-three fish with a total weight of 132 pounds gutted—an average of 6 pounds per fish gutted. So, the average real weight for these two-dozen blues was closer to 7-8 pounds each.

Based on the trip ticket records of the past, these were larger fish than past years.

I had also frozen several bluefish filets to bring home and smoke this winter.

At The Net Result, I placed my order for half a bushel of local Littleneck clams and ten boiled lobsters to take to my sister's for our annual end of the trip get together.

Then I turned right around an went back to Chappy in hopes of a repeating last night.

Guessed correctly. Bass fishing was the same as the night before. Guys taking pics of the beautiful moon. Bass inviting us to stay. Swirling and sweating and giggling to myself nonstop for ninety minutes. Having to remind myself to breathe now and then.

No keeper. No matter.

So much fun.

Aaron Carotta and two blues on the same lure.

Bill Moe with a bass from the Cape Pogue gut.

THE POWER OF GESTURE

Gestures matter.
As my trip began to end, I packed up everything I could a day early.

Emptied each room and put everything in the front room of the cottage except for my one bass rod, reel, waders. Filled the pockets of my raincoat with a headlight, a plastic case with a few lures, clippers, and extra leaders.

Did all this so that after a day of work at the computer, I could still go out to Chappy to fish that afternoon and night one more time.

Catching big bluefish on my light bass rod and releasing them toward the end of my annual trip had become a tradition. I was able to land and release three BIG blues in the afternoon. I savored every second of each hook up of a big blue on my light rod, releasing them instead of taking them to market.

I also savored one more time to share the beach with Island fishermen who have been so kind to me: Ralph Peckham, Jim Mullins, Sol Watson, Ron McKee, and Don Scarpone. They all are members of the Martha's Vineyard Surfcasters Association. You are welcome to join at *mvsurfcasters.org*. They would love to have you. I am a member myself.

There are gestures that matter.

All gestures signal something we hold to be important. Some gestures signal affection. Other gestures signal respect. Some gestures signal hope. Others signal integrity. Some gestures signal friendship. Others signal disappointment.

Gestures affirm something deeper than one can see or hear. You remember gestures more than words most of the time.

A few days ago, Ralph Peckham arranged for Ron Domurat and me to get a tour of the Shellfish hatchery in Vineyard Haven. Ralph knew that I had taken three aquaculture courses at my local community college back home so he wanted me to see the Island's remarkable hatchery. Made it his mission to set up the hatchery tour.

Notice Ralph's gesture.

(By the way, what looked like a half of teaspoon of sand at the bottom of a water tray was actually a thousand microscopic-sized clams. When you see one under the microscope you will never forget it.)

Today, each one of these Island fishermen made it a point to find me and say goodbye before leaving. Each knew my trip was ending. A gesture none of them had to make, but one that I will never forget. Each one could have just gone on their way after fishing this afternoon. But each one, on their own, made it a point before leaving to find me and say goodbye until next year.

Gestures matter.

That night, around 8 p.m., just before dusk, birds began diving in front us at the Rip. They were diving further out the night before when I asked Coop what they were eating.

"Squid," he said.

I have no idea how Coop knows this. But I know better than to doubt him.

So four of us fished under the diving birds for an hour and no one got even a hit.

At dark, Ron Domurat and I fished under the steps in front of the fishermen's parking lot like we had for the last three nights. I had parked there but Ron had parked "around the corner" back at the Rip.

I was able to catch three stripers between 9-9:30 p.m. All were just short at twenty-six to twenty-seven inches.

It would turn out to be the night I remembered most in the months to come. Not because of the good fishing but the way the full June moon shined on the dark sea. You could follow the drift of your line in the moonlight. The stars were gorgeous. The weather perfect.

Here, in this dark haven, I was far, far away from normal life. I was deep, *deep* into the best of night fishing life.

Ron was not so lucky.

He asked me about my luck and left me with a great irony as I was about to end my fishing trip.

"Ron, I've caught all my bass here on a bucktail without knowing how to jig it. I just sort of find the right speed to retrieve it. Must have to do with how deep it is in the water column and the speed of the current."

"Funny you should say that. Back in the '80s Al Spofford used to tell me the same thing. 'You don't have to jig a bucktail.'"

How ironic that after all these years I had come to discover a truth that my ole mentor Spoffy was trying to tell folks forty years ago. Spoffy's presence with me on this trip was unexpected.

Ron gave me a hug—another gesture—and said he would fish his way back "around the corner" toward the Rip and his parked car before heading home.

An early evening for me would mean I could get a few extra hours of sleep before starting my Last Day.

After exiting the Chappy ferry, I pulled over in front of the Memorial Wharf to pack up my waders and raincoat, enjoy a late-night cup of coffee, and stare at the glorious full moon. And one more thing to do.

There are a few hundred memorial bricks featuring the names of loved ones at the Memorial Wharf in Edgartown right next to the Chappy

Ferry. Got one for my dad when he passed away twenty years ago.

We place a piece of casting tape on his brick when we arrive every year as a way of having him join us.

I ended my trip with something my mom had come to appreciate over the years.

Before leaving, took off my hat, and with a touch and prayer, removed the tape on my dad's brick.

A gesture.

FISHING WITH GHOSTS

Ron McKee is from Maine and is the owner of Striper Maine-iac where he makes lures and builds rods that people love love love. He also might very well be on record for catching the most stripers over fifty pounds from shore and boat.

In making the time to say goodbye yesterday, we had this:

"Stay well, Ron. Hope you have a good summer!" I yelled.

"Oh yeah. I'll be out here fishing with ghosts!" he yelled back, smiling wide.

He saw me smile.

"Yep. Every night and every spot a different

person and a different memory: 'Hey Hawk, (the late beloved Hawkeye Jacobs) remember when we fished here back in … Think I should use this … or this?'

"'Hey Charlie, (not sure who) remember when we …'

"Every night a different person and every spot a different memory," he repeated.

"I know! I know!" I yelled. "And those are the real Keepers."

"What's that?" Ron yelled.

"THOSE ARE THE REAL KEEPERS!" I repeated a bit louder.

He nodded and grinned. The look in his eyes told me that he was so glad I understood.

This Spring trip, like every other one before it, includes fishing with the ghosts. Many of us know what this means. I suppose it is like that with most of the experiences we cherish and the traditions we maintain with all our heart.

On Chappy, I fished with ghosts of "different persons" in different spots like Ron said. Some deceased like Don Mohr, Arthur "Flash" Winters, Horace Johnson, Gary Tyson, Al Spofford, Ed Jerome, and Dad. And I fished with some not physically present but still breathing, like the

Zane family of fishermen, Paul Schultz, Jan and Joe Bals, and my son Ben who couldn't make it.

Ron McKee's ghosts also include "different memories" in different spots. My ghost memories included a trip down memory lane with Coop on Wasque at dusk, solitary nights "up Island" with Ben, early years in Lobsterville with Bernie and Dad, and days fishing Pogue Pond with the old timers.

Even recalled the time years ago when I ran into fisherman Jack Livingston, who came to the Island the same time as I did fifty years ago and stayed. In 2001 he won the Derby prize for largest shore blue with a fifteen-pounder. Several years ago we crossed paths on Chappy. Hadn't seen or spoken to Jack in years.

He rolls down the window and asks about something we have never ever mentioned to each other before. Doesn't say "Hello" or "Long time no see." No need to do all that with someone you have known and fished with on and off for that long. Besides, it doesn't matter with Jack. He has a knack for speaking straight away:

"So you figure out where you are going to be buried?"

"Got it down to two places," I quickly replied.

"Yeah. I got a spot picked out too. Just spread my dad's ashes down by the Elbow last year," said Jack.

"You doin' okay?" I asked.

"Doing great. My son just graduated from the high school here as Valedictorian. Going to Stanford on a free ride."

"Very cool. Take care Jack."

"You too."

"Good to see you."

"Yeah. You to. Always."

There are also a few fishing lessons learned on this trip that I hope to retain, but that remains to be seen:

A hard thing can be a good thing. Like those who complete a marathon, climb that rock, walk the Camino Way, grow and store a summer's worth of tomatoes, start a business, or learn a new language, doing something meaningful AND hard brings a sense of accomplishment and satisfaction.

Glad I did thirty straight. Won't again. No longer have to wonder what I will be missing if I rest one night when the wind blows hard North East or the tide and time don't match up in the one place I had my eyes on. Maybe try to skip those in the future instead of grinding through them.

Could go out together for ice cream or a lobster roll a couple of times. Maybe dinner at like a restaurant or something? Did that once about twenty years ago.

Sticking up for yourself sometimes is necessary. And sometimes it is best to let it roll off your back.

Trying something new—even if it takes twelve years of coaxing—is a good thing.

It is also a good thing to do most things the way you love to do them, even when there might be more effective and productive ways of doing them.

My life has been blessed by this annual experience and its Liminal space.

I suppose each of us can say this about our favorite place.

PART THREE
WHAT REMAINS

THE FISHING PARTNER

Picky.

You have to be super picky about who you go fishing with.

You and your fishing partner must have the same temperament, the same sensitivities, the same expectations, and the same level of patience.

Some surfcasting partners prefer to "chase" or "run and gun": fishing one spot for thirty or forty-five minutes and then another.

Others like to "camp out" or "park it": settling in a pre-ordained spot and fishing several hours during what they perceive to be the sweet spot in the tide.

It's challenging enough just to navigate tide, water, wind, and fish. Painful when one partner wants to run, the other wants to settle. Or one partner talks more or less than the other cares to. Or one wonders too much or too little about moving or staying or switching tactics or second-guessing choices. Or one analyzes and plans less or more than the other wants to.

And then there is the need for a like-minded level of satisfaction with the amount or lack of catch.

We never forget the discomfort and tension that comes from fishing with the wrong partners.

Finding the right partner sooner is way better than later.

And then there are a few who intentionally fish alone.

I have come to use the metaphor of "being picky with who I fish with" in the workplace as well. Not all of us have the luxury of deciding who we will work with on this project or that but the older I got, the more I would say this to colleagues and supervisors when suggestions were made as to who I might collaborate with.

People tend to understand. They get it—as long as you still are successful.

Then again, nothing is finer than finding a great fishing partner. Nothing. You have a companion who rolls at the same speed as you do, compatible in every way, sometimes adding just enough difference to keep things on balance or evolving.

And without a doubt, fishing partners derive as much joy from their partner's catch as they do their own.

I have been blessed with a family of perfect fishing partners. And there are traits common to all partners, fishing or otherwise:

Partners all have slightly different styles and favorite approaches.

Share the same expectations and appreciations.

Negotiate and discuss.

Give each other space.

Tease each other just enough.

Listen to each other's point of view.

Celebrate each other's success.

Enjoy the same spots, while each having their own favorite spot.

Love being with the other.

Know how to work with the other.

Are comfortable giving their opinion and

letting the other know when they will "sit this one out" to rest or soak in other aspects of this trip.

I have noticed over time how each of my fishing partners makes it a point to express appreciation for the shared experience of being together, of figuring things out, managing the ups and downs, and having fun.

And I wonder what it would be like if we all could express our appreciation a bit more to those we practice Keeping Company with on the water's edge, at the workplace, in our living room, or far away.

11:30 p.m. Chappy East Beach June 6, 2005.

Ben with a 35-pounder at Wasque June 6, 2004. 11:30 p.m. 40-year-old rod.

THE LAST DAY

The next morning ushered in the Last Day.

Truth be told, most of the visiting fishermen have to pack up and clean out their rental property and are not able to fish on The Last Day.

But deep down it is quite the opposite. We all fish on The Last Day.

You see, The Last Day lasts.

Lasts a year.

You don't fish the Last Day with a rod and reel. You fish it with memories and imagination.

With memory you actively recall certain sights, sounds, successes, mistakes, and conversation.

With imagination you dream of your return,

what you will do again, what you will be sure to savor, and what you will try differently.

You fish The Last Day on a Saturday morning four months later behind the steering wheel on your way to the grocery store.

You fish the Last Day watching TV at night and on an early morning walk.

You fish the Last Day in bed as you try to let go of the pressing matters of the day and hope to fall asleep.

You fish it mostly alone save for the occasional conversation with fishing partners.

You fish The Last Day until you are fortunate enough to experience a new First Day.

I'll say it again, The Last Day is not twenty-four hours. It's three hundred something days.

Isn't this the way it is on the Last Day of most vacations and adventures?

My Last Day always begins in the same way: a 6:30 a.m. visit to The Net Result for the clams and lobsters I have purchased with "the bluefish money in The Envelope", a sweet ferry ride back to the mainland, the transitional five-hour ride back to reality, and a fresh seafood feast at Angela's house.

But there is one more surprising gesture

awaiting as I begin my Last Day entering the back door of The Net Result for my clams and lobsters.

Lou Larsen himself has gotten up early to greet me. Lou sold the place the year before and retired. He had purchased our bluefish for nearly thirty years.

He had heard it was my Last Day and got up early to come see me before I left. We laughed and hugged and hung out for thirty minutes standing there in the back of The Net Result with Mike Holtham, the young prince of a fellow who now manages the place. Heartwarming in every sense of the word.

Lou didn't have to come by. Could've just said "Tell Mike I said, 'Hi.'" But he SHOWED UP.

Showing Up.

Sometimes this is the very best thing we can do for one another.

How much these gestures sustain us and matter to us.

I leave The Net Result and enter the line for the 7:30 ferry to Woods Hole. There is a text from Ron Domurat:

RON:

Walked into them near my car last night Mike.

Had a dozen fish slot size or better. Safe travels home my friend.

ME:

You got a dozen Keepers?

RON:

Yes, 25 total, all on bucktails. Had a fish on every cast for more than an hour. Best night in years!

ME:

That would have been around the exact time of the Moon rising.

RON:

Maybe. But they were spitting out squid.

I grinned big. After hugging goodbye last night, Ron walked into one of his best bass nights ever.

And ole Coop had said it was all about the squid.

On the Ferry back to daily life I took a count:

30 straight. 17 different places. 26 bluefish (3 to smoke over the Holidays) and around 60 stripers (7 keepers to be shared among 7 different families).

But it is not about the number of fish you keep. It about the moments, interactions, gestures, and experiences you take in and take home.

As the Last Day begins, I can see that my memory box is full of Keepers, captured on these pages.

- The two strangers who shared personal stressors or family legends while standing at the water's edge.
- Dick Pytko's story of the Vietnam vet giving away every one of his disability checks to the younger generation of veterans who needed it.
- The Log Day gift bluefish courtesy of Al Spofford and his forty-year-old orange lure.
- The first striper on the first night that sure enough spit the single hook Ben and Christin told me not to put on my lures.

- Overhearing Aaron Hurley, an elite fisherman, giggling out loud—alone—over a wonderfully large striper he caught and gently released.
- Guys in waders, fishing knee-deep in the surf, silently stopping to take photos of the sunset or moonrise.
- Eighty-six-year-old Ed Amaral with his head in my open passenger window making a case for Gratitude.
- The way the full moon shone on the water as I fished under the Fishermen's steps and had stripers on almost every cast.
- The evening in Lobsterville at a hallowed spot I last visited with Dad and Bernie Arruda and the way it looked as I left it—for the next generation.
- Twenty-four fly fishermen spaced out perfectly up at Lobsterville, with not a word said among them.
- The whippoorwill calls at the air hoses on the Chappy dirt road in front of Mytoi Gardens.

- The peaceful moments in the dark, enjoying the sights and sounds of the Edgartown harbor while waiting for the last Chappy Ferry and savoring a long day of casting.
- Billy Batterton and Steph Pond's generous tutorials on how to fish the bucktail.
- Coop giving me not one but three of his own bucktails.
- Spending quality time with the Shore Birds once again.
- Ninety-five-year-old Sid Siegel's description of trying to live the code his dad gave him when he was younger.
- Christin's company and good-natured teasing.
- The many gestures of grace from other fishermen.
- The hot soup to go from Morning Glory Farm.
- What a good muffin and hot coffee taste like at 9 p.m.
- Going through three loaves of sandwich bread and still losing ten pounds.

- The Jamaican seamstress in her shop across from the Black Dog in Vineyard Haven who sewed up the hole in the back of my favorite sweatshirt for ten dollars. She did not know what a sweatshirt was. Saw the large tear across the back collar (see cover photo) and wanted to know if a woman had gotten angry with me. Happily paid her twenty dollars.
- The way grisly fishermen fell over themselves to play with Phil Bibeau's cute little dog Piper.
- Ralph Peckham taking the time to arrange a field trip to the clam hatchery for me and Ron.
- The many nights fishing by myself on Chappy and noticing Jim Mullins' solitary light down the beach as if it was just the two of us on the whole Island.
- The pleasant, knowledgeable, and open way the new generation fishes.
- Bright and countless Stars in the sky that you don't see when near city lights.

- The way eighty-two-year-old Jake and his grandsons quietly, successfully fished their favorite spots in their favorite ways, no matter what the buzz was on the beach.
- Unsolicited texts from long-time Island fishermen like Ron D., Ralph, Janet, and Dick.
- The hard work, unrequited joy, and satisfaction of catching a striper you can keep and share with others.

MY BIGGEST KEEPER

And then there are some Keepers that should not be talked about.

Much.

It is as if, with each telling, they may lose some of the angel's stardust from which they come.

A tad of stardust given away with each telling until years later they no longer have the stardust they once had.

Except to the story's owner and friends whose hearts have enshrined it.

We all have some Keepers that should only be shared with those whom we Keep Company.

These Keepers are best shared only with those

who stand next to you and near you. Shared only with those who sit with you face-to-face and knee-to-knee when need be.

Or who ride in the passenger's seat of your life.

There are stories that should not be told.

Much.

They contain stories only shared late, after most of the other things that day have been handled.

Because they are too rich and righteous to waste on the fly.

Because they are too wholly human, wholly memorable, wholly intimate, wholly tender.

And like that.

Holy.

These stories should not be told.

Much.

In 2017, just after Christin and Ben had arrived on the Island, I turned around while fishing for blues in the Wasque Rip and noticed an antique Jeep Wagoneer parked behind me. It reminded me of the old Waggoneer Horace Johnson used to drive forty years ago when I was just learning how to fish. It was still there thirty minutes later when I pulled my line out to get a cup of coffee.

But the closer I got to this old Waggoneer, the quicker my pace.

Could this possibly be what I think it is? Sure looks a lot like Horace Johnson's old Waggoneer.

Sitting behind the steering wheel was a beloved old fisherman friend who was part of my past. I was nineteen when I first met him. He and all the other veterans used to call themselves Masters of The Beach. They were legendary surf fishermen, all of them. They were my idols. All year long I would dream of standing among them for two weeks of spring fishing.

Now, forty-five years later, they are all gone. But to my astonishment and joy, I am sure that one of them is sitting in his antique beach buggy right before me.

The man behind the wheel speaks to me through a half-rolled-down window.

"Listen," he says. "I drove all the way up here to see a few old friends and say goodbye before I die. I've met a few of them but I'm still looking for one guy. His name is Mike Caradid. Do you know—"

"Horace. It's me! Mike Carotta!" as I thrust my hand through the window's opening.

Ninety-one-year-old Horace Johnson, Horace N. Johnson, shook a little fog from his memory and squeezed my hand so tight I can still feel it.

"Oh, Mike. I have been telling people up here about you. Remember that time you took me to Lobsterville? I will never forget it. I was just hoping to run into you."

He climbed out of the car and we hugged.

Horace Johnson. Horace N. Johnson was referring to the time his old Waggoneer broke down and I offered to take him fishing with me that night to a legendary spot twenty-six miles away. We fished all night together in the dark. He loved it.

That was ten years ago.

When he was eighty.

We saw him again one time after that when he was almost eighty-five, but he could no longer stand in the surf. Shore birds P.J. Carr and Joe Cefalo took care of him, like the Zane brothers did years before that.

Horace fell in the ocean twice. Gone ever since.

Horace Johnson, Horace N. Johnson was a

proud man. Highly educated and articulate with an accomplished career helping RCA as it moved into the electronics lead. They actually gave him one of the first answering machines he helped develop. He gave it away.

"What the hell was I gonna do with it?" he once told me. "I didn't have people calling me. So I gave it to my brother-in-law. He loved it but he needed it even less than I did!"

Horace N. Johnson was also a throwback. A man's man. Not in the macho way but in the most noble of ways. Dignified. Strong.

Just like his rich baritone voice.

"My goodness Horace, I thought you were dead." I chuckled.

"Kinda wish I was. Lost my wife last year and I always thought I'd go first. Not the same man I was before she passed. Lost my heart you know."

"Sorry to hear that. Did you drive up here yourself?"

"Oh yeah. Ain't but six hours. I may be ninety-one but I can still drive. Came up here, like I said, to see a few guys and see this place one more time. Say goodbye before I die. First thing I did when I got here was go to the hospital and give them my information, in case I drop right here or get sick or something happened."

Pulled a white index card out of his shirt pocket. Had all his doctor's numbers on it as well as his prescriptions.

"Yeah after my wife passed, I lost my strength. Couple of years ago, I could kick your butt if I had to, you know. But now, no way."

His old Wagoneer was just like I remembered it. Organized and loaded with fishing gear.

"I was hoping to catch a fish one more time. You know. But I have trouble standing in the water now and it might be too much for me."

He came for one last trip. One three-day weekend.

He was staying with a friend of his family named Mario who was sitting next to him on the passenger side.

"I thought you were ninety-three?" Mario said.

"Nope. Ninety-one," said Horace.

"You look ninety-three."

"Shut up."

Mario couldn't fish a lick. Horace spent most of the first two days teaching him from the side of his jeep. But the strong wind and rough surf prevented Horace from fishing.

We talked a lot about old times. Mostly Horace would ask me if each of a dozen of the old spots were still productive and then we would take turns sharing old fishing stories about each of those spots. It was like he was checking to see if the places that had enriched his life were still the way he remembered them.

On the last day of the weekend, the wind had died down, the fish were close to the beach.

Perhaps within casting range for Horace. And he knew it. Of course he knew it.

I saw him sitting on his back tailgate, slowly trying to put on his waders.

"Lemme help you with that."

"No Mike. This is my test. If I can't get these on then I don't have any business fishing. If you can't cut the mustard, you shouldn't try to lick out the jar."

Ninety-one-year-old Horace got those waders on don't you know.

Of course he did.

He had three surf rods secured on his roof rack. Needed to get a key to open the old-school rack. Hands shook a little with that key and all. Told me he was gonna use the custom rod built to his specs.

"Rick Zane made it for me years ago. You remember Rick, right?"

Then Horace put on a thirty-year-old lure.

"Favorite lure right here. Gonna see if I can catch one more fish on my favorite lure right here."

"Horace, that lure won't cast as far as the new ones. Let me lend—"

"Came all this way to try and catch one more fish with this lure right here. No. But thank you."

We walked down to the surf together.

Slowly.

I stood behind him with my hand inches from his wader straps. He made few casts but not far enough to reach the fish. The surf's white water shifted the sand around his feet. He tried to hold his ground. Leaned forward face first toward the sea a few times but I was able to steady him. After five short minutes he realized he was not going to be able to do it and was ready to call it.

Horace Johnson, Horace N. Johnson was a proud man. But I took a calculated risk. What the heck I thought, he's calling it quits. I got nothing to lose.

"Horace … Would you mind if I cast one out for you?" I asked as gently as I could. His response caught me off guard.

"Would you be so kind?"

"Horace! Why the hell didn't you ask me to do this like, yesterday, man! I'm happy to do this! Are you kidding me?"

He was a little tired.

"That would be great, Mike."

"Alright, Horace. I'll cast it, but before the

lure even hits the water I'll hand you the rod while the lure is still in the air so you can work the whole thing even before it hits the water."

I practically attached myself to Horace's hip so I would be able pass him the rod. I reared back to cast, but checked with him one more time.

"You good?"

"I'm good."

"You ready?"

"Born ready."

We let it fly.

But there are some stories that should not be told.

Much.

Like what happened next.

A fish hit his thirty-year-old lure. Fisherman around him roared. Chaos surrounded us as people pulled their lines out of the water to watch. Some danced around us taking pictures. Horace was oblivious to all of it. Ninety-one-year-old Horace N. Johnson was in the moment he had come back for. While everyone shouted this or that, he quietly and calmly narrated the fish's fight at the end of his line.

"He's trying to go with the current," he said

calmly, holding steady. "There he is." He said a minute later as the fish got within view.

"Gonna turn him now," he said veteran-like as he prepared to pull him toward shore.

A LONG CAST

Just as he brought the fish to land, the rusted hook in the old lure broke off. Had it happened one second sooner the fish would have swam away.

Ben, anticipating things, had been following the fish onto the shore. He grabbed it just as the hook snapped off the lure and handed it to Horace Johnson. The old lure had given its owner his last fish.

The joy on that shore at that time among all those who were there came from another place.

It came as Gift and all knew it.

Horace N. Johnson.

But this is not a story about fishing or about Horace.

It's about doing a hard thing to bring something to closure.

Last Rights.

Repeat something in order to complete something.

Reconcile with the passing before it is gone.

Visit to say goodbye.

Return to that place, person, or activity for one last, sweet, soulful kiss.

It is not about stopping time or a vain demonstration that you still have it.

It is not even about nostalgia or sentimentality. It is not mushy or romantic.

Later, when all the celebration had subsided, I saw Horace sitting on the back of his tailgate, crying.

From the back, I saw his shoulders heaving up and down, waving his right hand at the fish in the sand.

It's about going back to a place
cause you from here
got roots here
worked here.
It's about going back to
Stand up one more time
Stand with one more time
Stand next to one more time.

It's about going to see someone or some place or some thing so as to

Touch home
Circle the bases
Pay respects.

About making a pilgrimage to a soulful place, a special person, a kindred group, or a life's keen endeavor.

Come Say Bye.

Horace had executed a soulful practice for us to replicate.

Come Say Bye

Some of us need to do it for closure so we can put it to rest.

Some of us need to do it in order to reconcile something still broken.

Some of us need to do it in order to properly give or pay respects.

We all have different reasons to do it.

Someone's about to be transferred or hospitalized.

The building we have history with is about to become a parking lot.

The musician who was part of the soundtrack of our life is about to go silent.

A thing we loved to do with all our heart is about to become impossible for us to do again.

Horace demonstrated that it is about going long in order to properly give thanks.

An extraordinary acknowledgment of what enriched our journey.

A humble handshake with whatever meant the world to you while you passed through it.

Holy like that.

Time and tide wait for no one. Life and love and laughter come harder as we age.

All of us have our reasons.

Right before our eyes, Horace had shown us how to

Come Say Bye.

These Keepers.

These sights, sounds, moments, experiences, encounters, and gestures that you are given. They abide within you and reappear long after they were caught.

You know what they are?

The best thing about fishing.

ACKNOWLEDGMENTS

Catherine Cronin Carotta. With all my heart I thank you for steadfastly making sure that we never stopped holding a lifetime of family gatherings here even when it did not seem feasible to do so.

Cover photo courtesy Benjamin Carotta.

In addition to all the other photos taken by family,

Photo of Joe Bals courtesy of Jan Bals

Photos of Lois Dimock, Billy Batterton, Bill Sr, Aaron Hurley, Steph Pond, and Bill Moe courtesy Billy Batterton.

Photo of Lance Dimock courtesy of Lois Dimock.

Photos of Jake Rudy and nephews Jeffrey and Peter courtesy of Paul "Jake" Rudy.

Photo of Ralph Peckham courtesy of Ralph Peckham.

Photos of Dick Millett and Polly Alden courtesy of Polly Alden.

Photo of Ron Domurat courtesy Ron Domurat.

Photo of Mike Carotta morning cast courtesy of Ron Domurat.

Many thanks also to Michael and Anthony Grasso, Larry Bressler, David Kasoff, PJ Carr, Sid Siegel, Joe Cefalo, Bernie Arruda, Ed Amaral, Cooper Gilkes, Phil Bibeau, and the late Horace N Johnson for allowing themselves to be photographed.

ABOUT THE AUTHOR

Mike Carotta is a lifelong religious educator and surfcaster who has driven to the Island every Spring from five different states over the years, including the last 21 from Omaha, Nebraska.

He and Catherine have recently moved to North Carolina where he has to adjust to a very different saltwater fishery.

He is now trying to make a decent pizza.

THANK YOU!

Thank you for reading! The team at Torchflame Books hopes you've enjoyed this book and might consider leaving a review on Amazon, Goodreads, BookBub, The Story Graph, or anywhere else you like to track your recent reads. Alternatively, you could post online or tell a friend about it. This helps our authors more than you may know.

Additional Large Print books are available for purchase at torchflamebooks.com/large-print or may be requested through your local library.

- The Team at Torchflame Books

www.ingramcontent.com/pod-product-compliance
Lightning Source LLC
Chambersburg PA
CBHW062012220426
43662CB00010B/1293